JESUS ON TRIAL

A Study in the Fourth Gospel

A. E. HARVEY

JOHN KNOX PRESS
ATLANTA

First published in Great Britain by SPCK in 1976
Published in U.S.A. by John Knox Press in 1977

©A. E. Harvey 1976

Biblical quotations are in general taken from The New English Bible,
second edition © 1970 by permission of Oxford and Cambridge
University Presses.

Library of Congress Cataloging in Publication Data
Harvey, Anthony Ernest.
   Jesus on trial.

   Reprint of the ed. published by SPCK, London.
   Bibliography: p.
   Includes indexes.
   1. Jesus Christ—Trial. 2. Bible. N.T.
John—Criticism, interpretation, etc. I. Title.
BT440.H37 1977   226'.5'06   77-79588
ISBN 0-8042-0335-0

Printed in the U.S.A.
John Knox Press
Atlanta, Georgia

Contents

Abbreviations

B.	Babylonian Talmud
Blass-Debrunner	*A Greek Grammar of the New Testament and other early Christian Literature,* tr. and ed. Robert W. Funk (1961)
Dodd, *Interpretation*	C. H. Dodd, *The Interpretation of the Fourth Gospel* (1955)
Dodd, *HTFG*	C. H. Dodd, *Historical Tradition in the Fourth Gospel* (1963)
e.	edition
ET	English Translation
JQR	*Jewish Quarterly Review*
JTS	*Journal of Theological Studies,* New Series
LSJ	*A Greek-English Lexicon,* by H. G. Liddell and R. Scott, revised by H. G. Jones
M.	Mishnah
Mek.	Mekilta
NEB	New English Bible
NTS	*New Testament Studies*
P.Ox.	Oxyrhynchus Papyri
R.	Rabbah
RHPR	*Revue d'Histoire et de Philosophie Religieuses*
RSV	Revised Standard Version
S-B	H. L. Strack and P. Billerbeck, *Kommentar zum Neuen Testament aus Talmud und Midrasch* (1922–8)
Suppl.	Supplement Volume
T.	Tosephta
TWNT	*Theologisches Wörterbuch zum Neuen Testament,* ed. G. Kittel and G. Friedrich (1933–)
VT	*Vetus Testamentum*
ZNW	*Zeitschrift für die Neutestamentliche Wissenschaft*

I

The Case of Jesus Christ

The earliest Christians had a 'gospel' to proclaim: that is to say, they had a message for mankind which promised joy, salvation, and hope to all who would receive it. This gospel concerned Jesus of Nazareth. And the most widely known fact about this Jesus was that which is still the most certainly known fact about him today: he was crucified by the Roman authorities in Jerusalem. The whole problem which confronted (and still confronts) any preacher or Gospel writer stemmed from this single fact. How could one who was known to have met his death in this way possibly be the subject of a Gospel, of 'good news'?

From the theological point of view, the bare statement that 'Jesus was crucified under Pontius Pilate' is a sufficient starting-point for the problem posed by Christianity: the fact *that* Jesus was put to death is all important and the details of how this happened may seem trivial.[1] But from the point of view of history, the statement has important implications which deserve to be spelled out. Jesus was crucified: that is to say, he was put to death by a form of execution which was not recognized in Jewish Law,[2] but which was normally used by the Romans (and other rulers) as a punishment for brigands and insurrectionaries.[3] This took place, not as an act of war,

---

[1] But recently systematic theology has begun to show more interest in the details, cf. J. Moltmann, *The Crucified God* (1974).

[2] Though there is some evidence for its occasional application by Jewish courts, cf. E. Bammel in E. Bammel, ed., *The Trial of Jesus* (1970), 162–5.

[3] Josephus, *Vita* 420; *B.J.* II, 253; *Ant.* xx, 102.

but in time of peace;[4] consequently it must have been preceded
by an official trial conducted by the Roman governor himself.[5]
Proceedings of this kind might possibly have been initiated by
the Romans. Jesus could have been arrested by Roman police
action and tried on a charge of insurrection. The appearance of
Roman military terms (*speira*, meaning cohort, and *chiliarchos*,
meaning tribune) in the account of Jesus' arrest in the Fourth
Gospel (18.12) has occasionally led critics[6] to think that this
is what happened to Jesus. But the unanimous testimony of the
New Testament writers is that proceedings were initiated by
the Jews—which would have been the more normal procedure;
and this is accepted by the great majority of modern scholars.

The single statement, therefore, that Jesus was crucified
implies others of equal historical reliability: Jesus underwent
a trial before the Roman governor, and was condemned to
death on a charge laid by Jewish informers. What was this
charge? We have seen that the manner of his execution was
one normally reserved for brigands and insurrectionaries (two
of whom were actually crucified beside him, Mark 15.27). But
there is a further piece of evidence. It was normal[7] to write
on the cross the charge on which the victim had been condemned (the *titulus*). In the case of Jesus, this has been recorded: 'Jesus of Nazareth, King of the Jews'. Our witnesses
to the second clause of this charge are unanimous; and (since
it was vitally important to Christians to show that their Lord
had *not* aspired to be a secular king) they are most unlikely to
have invented it, and indeed must have felt it to be embarras-
sing. It is therefore almost certainly authentic. And the words
it contains deserve further comment.

[4] Relative, of course. A 'rising' is refered to in Mark 15.7; but
only full-scale war or rebellion would have justified summary
execution.

[5] Technically called *cognitio*, cf. A. N. Sherwin-White, *Roman
Society and Roman Law in the New Testament* (1963), 23.

[6] e.g. O. Cullmann, *Jesus und die Revolutionären seiner Zeit* (1970),
49–50; P. Winter, *The Trial of Jesus* (1961), 129–30.

[7] cf. Arndt and Gingrich, *Lexicon* s.v. τίτλος.

From the point of view of the Roman government, such a charge is perfectly plausible. Brigands who aspired to the kingship had been rife in the tumultuous years which followed the death of Herod the Great,[8] and similar aspirations are ascribed to the Jewish rebel Menahem in A.D. 66.[9] An insurrectionary could perfectly well have been crucified on this charge in the intervening period. Moreover, it is likely that the Jewish authorities, in their anxiety to keep the peace, would have been ready to bring one of their compatriots before the governor on such a charge. This is doubtless what happened in the case of Jesus. The difficulty is that, to have been accepted by Pilate, the charge must have seemed plausible. The royal pretender must have attracted sufficient support to be capable of offering a real threat to the Roman government. He must have had a private army or, at the very least, a considerable retinue of armed men. Virtually[10] nothing that we know about Jesus fits this portrait at all.[11] Laid against Jesus, the charge seems totally implausible.

We are apparently faced with a contradiction. On the one hand, the events and legal procedures leading up to Jesus' death can be established with reasonable certainty as implications of the bare statement that he was crucified; and the charge upon which he was crucified is given by a report which, again, seems highly reliable: King of the Jews. On the other hand, it seems incredible that the person condemned on this charge was Jesus of Nazareth. Either we have a totally dis-

[8] Josephus, *B.J.* II, 55.

[9] ibid., II, 444.

[10] The two swords belonging to his followers in Gethsemane are the total complement of Jesus' armed support.

[11] Certain writers have exploited in this connection Jesus' association with zealots. But the zealots were out to establish a theocracy, not a new royal line. No zealot would have allowed himself to be suspected of such pretensions. cf. S. G. F. Brandon, *Jesus and the Zealots*, 48f. Moreover, the very existence of a zealot party and of widespread 'zealot' activity in Jesus' lifetime has recently been called into question. cf. M. Borg, *JTS* 22 (1971), 504–12; P. W. Barnett, *NTS* 21 (1975), 564–71.

torted picture of Jesus, or the charge was unfounded and the conviction unjust.

At this point, however, we must introduce a complicating factor. Palestine, in the time of Jesus, had not one legal system but two.[12] There were the courts set up by the secular power to hear all cases concerned with matters which in any way affected government (public order, taxation, etc.); and there were the courts and judicial procedures which the Jews had inherited from the days of their independence and which were still permitted by the foreign authority to settle disputes in private law and in all matters which we would now call 'religious'. These two jurisdictions inevitably overlapped, and could be played off against each other by unscrupulous citizens.[13] In particular, Jewish law prescribed the death penalty for certain crimes, but the power to inflict it was reserved to the governor,[14] and then only after a hearing in his own court. If the charge against Jesus, that he was or claimed to be 'king of the Jews', originated in a Jewish court, it could have had very different and much more plausible connotations.

This, as is well known, is the solution to our difficulty which is offered by the Gospels. Jesus was found guilty by a Jewish court of claiming (or admitting) to be a person who could be variously described as 'Son of God' or 'Messiah'. Such a claim or admission (assuming, as Jesus' judges were bound to do, that it was not true) could be interpreted as blasphemy,[15] and this, under Hebrew law, was punishable by death. To obtain (as was necessary under the prevailing 'condominium') a verdict from the governor's court, a charge couched in such esoteric terms would have been useless. Fortunately, one popular[16] description of this personage whom Jesus allegedly claimed

[12] cf. J. D. M. Derrett, *Jesus's Audience* (1973), 87–93.

[13] Derrett, *NTS* 18 (1972), 182–3.

[14] This has been hotly disputed by theologians. But the judgement of professional historians (Mommsen, *ZNW* 3 (1902), 199; A. N. Sherwin-White, op. cit., 35–43) seems decisive.

[15] This point is discussed in detail below, pp. 77–81.

[16] It is used by the crowds of Jesus in Luke 19.38; 23.37; Matt. 27.42.

to be was 'King'. Of course, to the Jews this title might mean something very different from an ordinary claimant to, or usurper of, a political throne; but at least it was the kind of term a pagan would understand, and on this charge the enemies of Jesus secured his conviction in the only court that was competent to carry out the death penalty.

So, at least, the matter is presented in the Synoptic Gospels (though somewhat differently in the Fourth Gospel, as we shall see). This presentation has come under formidable criticism from scholars; but at least it may be said to offer a solution to the dilemma created by a fact which may be inferred with certainty from Jesus' crucifixion and from the *titulus* on the cross: the fact that Jesus was convicted in a Roman court on a charge of being, or claiming to be, 'King of the Jews', even though nothing in the record about Jesus seems to bear out such a charge. In the absence of a better solution, it may be allowed to stand for the present. Let us return to the task which confronted the first preachers and Gospel writers.

This task can now be seen to have been somewhat harder than appeared at first. The message to be proclaimed was that salvation had been obtained for men through Jesus. But Jesus had been crucified: how could he then have been a person from whom flowed such effects? Had Jesus' condemnation been the work of a pagan court only, there would have been little difficulty. Such courts had no high reputation (among the Jews) for justice.[17] Only the contravention of Roman administrative law need have been involved, and many pious Jewish patriots of unimpeachable righteousness under the Jewish law might have incurred a similar fate. A verdict recorded by such an authority need have had no serious implications for the claims made for Jesus, which were of an order which passed right out of the cognizance of any Roman magistrate.[18] But the situation was startlingly different if it was the

---

[17] J. D. M. Derrett, *NTS* 18 (1972), 184. The arbitrator in such a court was a κριτὴς τῆς ἀδικίας.

[18] As was the case before Gallio—Acts. 18.15.

case that Jesus was also tried before a Jewish court. For here, there would be a strong presumption (at least in the minds of Jewish readers) that the court was right! The law which it was applying to this particular case was the Torah, the revealed justice of God; and its procedures (particularly if it was a central court under the presidency of the High Priest) were also normally above suspicion. If such a court found Jesus guilty on a capital charge, either Jesus must have been properly condemned in the sight of God (which the resurrection showed not to have been the case) or else, in some way, the system itself must have been at fault. Paul seems to have been prepared to follow the logic of this to its conclusion, when he acknowledged that Jeus had been made 'sin', 'a curse', in the eyes of the law, and that this cast doubt upon the whole of the existing legal system (the Torah—Gal. 3.13). The authors of the Synoptic Gospels adopt a less radical line: the hearing of Jesus' case was conducted so perfunctorily that it barely amounted to a judicial process at all. Only in John, as we shall see, is the case for and against Jesus argued out at length, so that the reader has to make up his own mind and form his own judgement.

What is it precisely about which the reader of a Gospel does have to make up his mind? John's Gospel is the only one of the four to offer an explicit answer to this question, though this answer would fit the other three equally well. Right at the end of the Gospel stand the words, 'In order that you may hold the faith[19] that Jesus is the Christ, the Son of God' (20.31). These words contain a paradox, which may easily escape a modern Christian, but which would have struck at once a contemporary Jewish reader.[20] To a Jew, the term 'Christ' meant a figure of power and glory. When such a person

[19] Or 'come to believe'. A tantalizing uncertainty in the textual tradition between πιστεύητε and πιστεύσητε makes it impossible to infer from this passage whether the readers are envisaged as believers or unbelievers.

[20] It is indeed the main burden of Justin's dialogue with the Jew Trypho in the second century A.D.

came, it would hardly be possible not to be aware of the fact. His reign would be marked by decisive victories over the enemies of the Jewish people: it would be absurd to think of writing a book to prove that he had come! Christians, however, were not deterred from calling Jesus 'Christ'. Whether or not he had actually accepted this title while on earth, his followers now knew that his continuing power among them was explicable only if he were indeed a person endued with such power and authorization that it was appropriate to call him Christ. Their problem was only that which is put into the mouth of Judas (not Iscariot) in John's Gospel: 'Lord what can have happened that you mean to show yourself to us alone and not to the world?' (14.22).

In part, this was felt by the early Christians to be no more than a matter of time. It would not be long before 'every eye would see him, even those who had pierced him' (Rev. 1.7). The Christ would return in glory. But from the start there was also a recognition of a certain *necessity* that the Christ must encounter indifference, blindness, and rejection. Remembering some fragments of Jesus' teaching, and applying (for the first time) some Old Testament prophecies to this Coming One which spoke not only of glory but also of suffering, they began to find in Scripture a confirmation of what had seemed one of the most startling aspects of their faith: 'Was the Messiah not bound to suffer thus before entering upon his glory?' (Luke 24.26).

It is in these terms that we can see Mark's Gospel in particular (and Matthew's and Luke's each in its own way) offering an answer to the question why the Christ was rejected by all but his few followers—and why, therefore, it was necessary to write a 'Gospel' to show that he had come. The same question occupies the writer of the Fourth Gospel; but the Prologue makes it clear that the question will have to be answered at a different level. In the understanding of this writer (and doubtless of a large number of the Christians of his generation) Jesus was very much more than a man who could be described by a term so limited, so relatively parochial, as 'the Christ'.

Jesus was a figure who far transcended the somewhat narrow and nationalist categories of Jewish religious expectation. He was the Saviour, not just of one people, but of all people. He gave meaning, not only to human life, but to the whole created order. His life was no isolated phenomenon: there was, so to speak, a *Jesus principle* built into the universe—the Logos. But if so, the problem of his rejection became more acute than ever, and more far-reaching. If 'through him all things came to be, and no single thing was created without him' (1.3), how was it possible for men not to recognize him for what he was? The paradox had to be stated in much wider terms than those which described merely the rejection and suffering of a Messiah: 'The world, though it owed its being to him, did not recognize him. He entered his own realm, and his own would not receive him' (1.10–11).

Nevertheless, even to state the paradox in these general terms is to approach the matter from a distinctively Christian point of view. Most Jewish people certainly expected a Messiah; and the Christians believed that this Messiah had now come in the person of Jesus. To support this belief, it was inevitable that they should have kept the two terms, Jesus and Messiah, in the centre of the argument. Any scriptural prophecy which seemed to be fulfilled in Jesus, any word or deed of 'messianic' significance, was eagerly drawn into the debate as evidence for the basic proposition that Jesus is the Christ, and modern scholars have devoted much research to the question whether the various titles used by, or of, Jesus would have been regarded by his contemporaries as identifying him with the expected Messiah. But it seems that this concentration upon a person, rather than on the state of affairs in which such a person would have a part to play, derives more from the inevitable Christian preoccupation with the nature and status of Jesus, than from the speculations and beliefs of his Jewish contemporaries. That most Jews of his time looked forward to the coming of the Messiah is certain. But this expectation was always part of a larger hope. The primary and dominant element in Jewish thinking about the future was always a new and splendid state of affairs, when the sovereignty of God and the rightful place of his chosen people would be unambiguously revealed to the world. The dawning of this new age was commonly associated with a figure who would act as God's instrument. This figure was usually the Messiah; but others (such as 'The Prophet', Elijah, or Moses) were frequently mentioned in the same context. The Jewish writings of the period present no ordered and systematic picture; the precise form of these expectations varies from writer to writer. But, whether one looks at apocalyptic, at rabbinic literature, or at subsequent Jewish tradition, one principle is constant: the primary emphasis is on the new state of affairs which is to be brought about by God. The identity and character of the person who will be instrumental in effecting this change is secondary.[21]

An important corollary of this principle is that the claim which it seemed so important to Christians to establish (that the Messiah had come) would not have seemed the primary one to Jews. They would have asked first (as they still do) whether the messianic age had come; only then would it have been appropriate to seek to identify the Messiah or the Prophet who had been instrumental in bringing it about. It follows that no one would have given any credence to a man who claimed to be Messiah regardless of any observable change in the course of history. The first recorded 'Pseudo-Messiah' or messianic pretender was Bar Koziba (A.D. 135); after him there was not another until Abu Isa al-Ispahani, who led a rebellion against the Umayyad Caliph in the eighth century A.D. The 'Pseudo-Christs' referred to in Matthew 24.24 as features of the last days seem to be a product of the Christian

[21] cf. D. S. Russell, *The Method and Message of Jewish Apocalyptic* (1964), 309–10: 'The emphasis is not so much on the Messiah and his ushering in of the Kingdom as it is on the Kingdom itself ...'. The same is true of Tannaitic Judaism (J. Klausner, *Messianic Idea* (ET 1956), 458f) and of Philo (H. A. Wolfson, *Philo*, II, 407–15). For a modern statement, cf. Leo Baeck, *The Essence of Judaism* (ET 1936), 250; J. Petuchowski in *Concilium*, N.S. vols. 7/8, no. 10 (1974), 150–5.

rather than the contemporary Jewish imagination.[22] Of course, the appearance of a man with unusual powers would arouse interest, since the arrival of the Messiah would doubtless be one of the signs by which the new age would he heralded. The question asked of John the Baptist, 'Are you the Messiah?', would have been perfectly natural under the circumstances. But the notion that a man would have gone about Palestine claiming to be the Messiah regardless of any observable changes in the fortunes of the people,[23] or that the question whether a person *was* the Messiah could be settled by reference only to his character and not to the whole context in which he appeared, would have been as alien to Jesus' Jewish contemporaries as it is to Jewish people today.

That the emphasis shifted to the person of Jesus in the minds of early Christian preachers and writers is understandable. But in the teaching of Jesus himself we find little concentration on his own individual significance. Rather (as we should expect) he draws attention to the new state of affairs which it is his function to inaugurate. 'Repent; for the Kingdom of God is at hand' is the manifesto which the synoptic evangelists place at the head of his teaching; and it is obvious to any reader of the Gospels that it is indeed the Kingdom, and not his own person, which stands at the centre of his teaching, of his parables, and indeed of all his activity. Jesus does, of course, say important things about himself; but his characteristic way of doing so is to use a form of words beginning 'The Son of Man ...'. Immense research has gone into the question whether this phrase is to be understood as a

---

[22] They have also sparked off the imagination of NT scholars, who have been too ready to assume that 'messianic pretenders' were a frequent occurrence in the first half of the first century A.D. None of the rebel leaders mentioned by Josephus claimed to be anything more than a 'king'. The view of M. Hengel, *Victory over Violence* (ET 1975), 55, n.61 that Josephus was deliberately suppressing all notice of Jewish messianic hopes is unconvincing, particularly in the light of *Ant.* XVII, 285.

[23] cf. B. Sanh. 93b: Bar Koziba claimed to be the Messiah, but only after he had 'reigned 2½ years'.

designation for the Messiah; but it would seem to be more in keeping with the whole tenor of Jesus' teaching and with the intellectual climate in which he gave it that this phrase should have a kind of deliberate evasiveness and ambiguity[24] than that it should embody a claim to be a specific figure in the unfolding of God's purpose. Indeed, if anything is characteristic of Jesus' teaching in the Synoptic Gospels,[25] it is that he appears continually to be diverting attention away from himself to the situation which his coming has provoked. A singularly eloquent example of this is his conversation with the emissaries of John the Baptist (Matt. 11.2–6). To their question, whether he is the expected person, he replies by pointing to the phenomena taking place around him which might be signs of the messianic age. In this, he seems to have aligned himself faithfully with the popular expectation of his time. Again and again, the essence of his teaching is, not a claim to a special role and status for himself, but an invitation to see the signs of a dawning kingdom in the responses of men to his message and in the events of contemporary history.

This emphasis on the Kingdom rather than the King, on circumstances rather than a person, is faithfully presented in much of the synoptic record. Christians were claiming that the promised New Age had come: and the Synoptic Gospels furnished them with arguments to use against those who doubted this claim. The very fact that this new age, if indeed it had come, had not been widely recognized to have come by the Jews (who so devoutly hoped for it) made it vitally

[24] The argument of G. Vermes (in M. Black, *An Aramaic Approach to the Gospels and Acts*, (3e., 1967), 310–30) that 'Son of Man' was an Aramaic idiom used by Jesus as a deliberate and modest circumlocution for the pronoun 'I' has not yet been widely accepted by scholars, but it gains plausibility in the light of what is said above. See also Vermes' reply to his critics in *Jesus the Jew* (1973), 188–91. The ambiguity of the expression was apparent to a Jewish scholar such as J. Klausner, *Jesus of Nazareth* (ET 1925), 257.

[25] It reappears also in John, notably in 3.2–3 where Nicodemus addresses Jesus as a 'teacher sent from God', and Jesus answers with a discourse on how to enter the Kingdom of God.

necessary to be able to show how different the Kingdom of God was from the crude expectations which are so often revealed in Jewish writings; and for this purpose Jesus' teaching about the Kingdom was of immense interest and importance. From this point of view, too, one can see the urgency which lay in the task assumed by Luke in writing Acts: that of demonstrating how the early history of the Church revealed a new state of affairs, the new age foretold by the prophets.

Yet this new age could not possibly be proclaimed except in relation to Jesus. It was entirely through him that God had brought it about; and it was inevitable that an argument with anyone who disbelieved the Christian proclamation should come to turn on the person of Jesus himself. If the new age had come (or was now coming), then Jesus was the agent uniquely appointed by God to bring it about. He must be (though he was also more than this) one of those figures whom Jewish expectation imagined to be essential for the working out of God's purpose: the Prophet, or Elijah, or (most likely of all) the Messiah. On the strength of numerous texts in the Old Testament (and perhaps of some words of Jesus himself) Christians from the first unhesitatingly pronounced him to be the Messiah, so much so that his name quickly became 'Jesus Christ'. In doing so, they made it certain that the argument should return to the question about Jesus: was he or was he not the Messiah? Was it or was it not the case that he had spoken and acted as God's agent and with God's authorization? And we find that John's Gospel was explicitly intended to answer this question (20.31).

We have seen that a major obstacle to the acceptance of the Christian claim was that Jesus had been found guilty on a capital charge by a competent Jewish court (this we have found to be a secure inference from the facts of the crucifixion and the *titulus*). If, in the eyes of the law (the revealed law of God), Jesus was found to have committed an offence justifying the death penalty, how could he possibly have been a person authorized by God to do and say what he did? How could he have been the Messiah, or indeed any person about whom prophecies were made in that same law? One answer might be that the law was not in fact brought to bear properly upon this case at all: the judges were so hard pressed by political considerations that their judgement was totally corrupt. As we shall see, this appears to be the line taken for the most part in the Synoptic Gospels. But it was certainly not the view taken by all Christians. We have already noticed that Paul seems to have been ready to accept the possibility that Jesus had been properly condemned under the law: as a result, the law itself was called into question. But it would have been possible to put the matter less theoretically. According to Jewish procedure (as will be explained later), a man's accusers might also be his judges; and to ask whether he had been rightly condemned would be to ask to hear the arguments of the prosecution and the counter-arguments of the accused—in short, it would be to ask that the dispute between the parties should be laid before the reader, so that he could make up his own mind who was in the right. It is in this light that we shall find we can best understand the series of disputes which are recorded in John's Gospel between Jesus and 'the Jews'.

It might be thought that there is something artificial about expressing the matter in such legal terms. The title Messiah was a religious and perhaps political one. Whether a person could lay claim to such a title surely depended upon his character and his exploits. His contemporaries were surely free to make up their own minds about him; why subject the issue to the precise definitions required in a court of law? But this would be to misunderstand the part played by the law in Jewish life and Jewish religion. Consider the following verses from Deuteronomy (18.18–20):

I will raise up for them a prophet like you, one of their own race, and I will put my words into his mouth. He shall convey all my commands to them, and if anyone does not listen to the words which he will speak in my name I will require satisfaction from him. But the prophet who presumes to utter in my name what I have not commanded him or who speaks in the name of other gods—that prophet shall die.

Such a person, then, 'a prophet', was due to appear; but his appearance would be fraught with legal consequences. If men failed to attend to his words, they would be committing an offence; but if, on the other hand, the prophet was an impostor, he must be condemned to death. To establish whether the 'prophet' was true or false would, therefore, be an urgent matter if those who heard him were to avoid the risk of committing a serious offence in the eyes of the law. And not only a prophet: anyone who gave teaching which was at variance with tradition (as the Messiah might do, and as Jesus certainly did) would be incurring the risk of death under the law: 'Anyone who presumes to reject the decision either of the priest who ministers there to the Lord your God, or of the judge, shall die' (Deut. 17.12)—a risk which was certainly not a dead letter in the time of Jesus.[26] To anyone with knowledge of Jewish law, the appearance of Jesus would have immediately raised issues of a strictly legal nature.

That the author of the Fourth Gospel did have such knowledge, and that he clearly appreciated the legal issues raised, will become apparent in the following chapters. It will be seen that a number of episodes in the Gospel are deliberately reported in the form of legal proceedings and that characteristic Johannine terms such as 'evidence' and 'witness' have their full technical force. Put rather crudely, the difference between the synoptic and the Johannine treatment of 'the case of Jesus' is that, in the Synoptic Gospels, the question is 'Why was Jesus delivered up to the Romans to be put to death?', and the answer is sought in political or psychological terms (through ignorance—Acts 3.17; 13.27; through envy—Mark 15.10); whereas in the Fourth Gospel the issue is more formal and clear cut: given that Jesus was (as a matter of history) con-

---

[26] M. Sanh. 11.2–3; T. Sanh. 11.7 (recording a difference on procedure between two second-century rabbis).

demned to death by men fully competent in the Law of Moses, who was right, he or they?

Stated thus, the difference is exaggerated. We shall find traces in the Synoptic Gospels of an appreciation of the legal consequences of Jesus' words and actions, and there are approaches in John's Gospel, other than strictly legal ones, to the question why Jesus was put to death.[27] Yet it must strike every reader of this Gospel that disputes between Jesus and 'the Jews' occupy a large part of the narrative, and when it is seen that these disputes have much of the formal character of a case at law, then it becomes a fair description of substantial sections of the Gospel to say that they constitute an argument, laid out before the reader for his judgement, designed to show which of the protagonists was in the right.

All this is evidence (as we shall see) not only of accurate knowledge of Jewish legal procedure, but of an utterly Jewish mentality. Indeed, this mentality is revealed, not only in the grasp of procedural details, but in the literary composition of the Gospel itself. The underlying pattern, as we have seen, is of two parties in dispute, Jesus and 'the Jews'; and the dispute has to be presented in such a way that the reader is persuaded of the justice of Jesus' cause. Clearly (as is evident, for instance, from the Synoptic Gospels) this was not the only way of presenting to the reader the challenge constituted by the person of Jesus. One does not have to imagine two parties quarrelling and indulging in counter-accusations in order to assess the claims of Jesus upon one's assent and one's allegiance. But Hebrew practice, and consequently Hebrew literature, allowed more matters to come to court, or at least to be discussed as possible subjects of litigation, than would naturally be the case in the western world.[28] Not only so, but this fundamental model of two parties in dispute at law entered the realm of religious thought, so that it seemed a natural

[27] Note especially the reasoning attributed to Caiaphas—11.49–53.
[28] cf. the general survey of this in the Old Testament in B. Gemser, *The Ribh-pattern in Hebrew mentality (Suppl. VT* III, 1955), 120–37.

form of expression to represent man as accusing God of injustice in allowing certain things to happen,[29] and God as bringing a formal accusation against his people for their disloyalty. This tendency to present an issue under the literary form of a trial or dispute (a *ribh*)[30] must be borne in mind when we come to consider how far the disputes recorded in John's Gospel are intended to be understood as records of actual legal proceedings, or how far they are rather literary elaborations of issues which were known to be in dispute between Jesus and the Jews (that of healing on the sabbath, for instance). But there is a further and very suggestive resemblance which may be noted at once. The speeches of the parties to such a dispute were very different from what would have been expected, say, in a western court. There was no attempt to build up a case bit by bit, accumulating evidence by stages and giving the whole presentation a logical cogency of its own. Rather it was a matter of each party stating his case again and again in such a way as to dispel the doubts of his listeners.[31] The object was not so much to present a *case* which could not be demolished as to present oneself as a *person* who deserved to be believed; and the most effective way of achieving this was often to say the same thing over and over again, with only small variations of detail, and with repeated insistence upon one's own credentials. It will be seen at once

---

[29] This began with Israel's collective complaints against God (e.g. Exod. 17.2), or those of their representative (Deut. 1.9–12), and developed into the longing for justice felt by an individual such as Job or the author of some of the psalms. cf. Gemser, loc. cit., 133–5.

[30] The *ribh*-pattern in such passages as Deut. 32; Isa. 1; Jer. 2; Mic. 6; and Ps. 50 has been intensively studied, most recently by J. Harvey, *Le Plaidoyer prophétique contre Israel après la rupture de l'alliance* (1967), who argues, however, that the origin of this literary form is to be found, not in the procedures of civil law, but in the ultimatum of a king against a state which has broken a sacred alliance.

[31] 'Before the legal assembly the speech and counterspeech continue back and forth until one party has nothing more to say.' L. Köhler, *Hebrew Man* (ET 1956), 159–60.

that this description fits many of Jesus' discourses in the Fourth Gospel.[32]

In this sense, then, it is possible to understand the Fourth Gospel as a presentation of the claims of Jesus in the form of an extended 'trial'. In part, this may be seen as a literary device: it was by rehearsing the arguments of the claimant against his adversaries before an imaginary court that Hebrew writers had deepened their readers' understanding of the 'righteous case' of God against his people or of an innocent man such as Job against his calumniators; similarly the evangelist could take the claims to be made for Jesus as an opportunity to focus attention on the witnesses and the arguments which were relevant. But in this case the device was by no means artificial. Jesus had, as a matter of historical fact, been tried before a competent court, and had in addition committed acts and spoken words which were fraught with legal consequences. In devoting so much of his Gospel to these incidents, the writer may have been doing no more than selecting such material from the traditions about Jesus as would enable him to present the case of Jesus Christ to his readers and challenge them—as the world has been challenged ever since—to reach their own verdict.

[32] The literary similarities between the Fourth Gospel and the Book of Job are well summarized by O. Betz, *Der Paraklet* (1963), 122-3, who draws, however, somewhat different conclusions from them.

2

The Witnesses in the Case

JOHN THE BAPTIST

The Fourth Gospel opens with a magnificent series of apparently metaphysical propositions. The time is the beginning of all things, the theme is the creation, and the substantives denote a sequence of large concepts: God, the word, light, life, darkness. To the consternation of commentators, the sequence is interrupted, after only five verses, by an isolated and highly particular historical statement: 'There was a man sent from God, whose name was John.' An explanation of this statement is given in the very next sentence: 'This man came for the purpose of giving evidence, to witness to the light'; and the theme that this was indeed the purpose of John's appearance is consistently maintained in the following chapters. 'This is the evidence John gave' is the heading of the very next section (1.19); two further references to the Baptist expressly mention his evidence and the weight it carried (1.20, 32); and there is a striking tendency for his pronouncements to be phrased, not as pieces of new information, but as repetitions of previous statements. 'This is he about whom I said ...' (1.30), 'I saw, and gave my evidence' (1.34), 'You yourselves can testify that I said ...' (3.28). It is as if, rather than proclaiming something new, John the Baptist is at each new turn of events made to show how the evidence he originally gave receives fresh and impressive confirmation. In short, the theme of John the Baptist as a witness penetrates deeply into the Gospel. The only surprise is that it appears so abruptly and so near the beginning. Recent commentators have mostly found it inconceivable that it could have belonged to the original form of the prologue or its source, and assume that

18

the evangelist inserted it subsequently.[1] But it is worth recalling that it is only recent scholarship which has reacted in this way. Westcott, for example, though he admitted that the introduction of John the Baptist is 'abrupt', nevertheless felt that it could be satisfactorily explained as a stage in the evangelist's argument.[2] The question whether, in the particular perspective of this Gospel which we propose to explore, this verse occupies a logical place in the prologue, is one with which we may begin our study of 'the witnesses in the case'.

Two points must be made at the outset. The first is the very obvious one that John the Baptist could not in any case have appeared in any place but at the beginning. In all four Gospels, in the sermons recorded in Acts, and indeed in the standard pattern of early Christian proclamation (so far as we can reconstruct it) the figure who appears at the opening of the Christian story is, not Jesus, but John the Baptist. Presumably these first Christian preachers and writers had no real choice in the matter. It was true that the unique and decisive event which was the main subject matter of any sermon and any Gospel was the coming of Jesus. But it was also true that this had been preceded by another event, in itself equally unprecedented and arresting: the coming of John the Baptist. So close were these two figures in time, so intimately connected were their activities, that it was impossible to tell the story of Jesus without reference to John. Thus far, all were agreed. But further questions then began to emerge. What was the precise relationship between the work of these two? What was the actual significance of John the Baptist's less vivid and sensational, but still clearly important, activity? What was it which assured him his inevitable place at the beginning of the Christian story? To this the answer of the three Synoptic

---

[1] e.g. Bultmann: 'a note inserted by the evangelist'; Barnabas Lindars, *Behind the Fourth Gospel*, 15: 'It is scarcely possible to believe that it belongs to the original form of the prologue.' C. K. Barrett (*The Prologue of St John's Gospel*, 1971) now takes a different view, but his reasons are different from those advanced here.

[2] *St John* (1880) ad loc.

Gospels (even if they differ in small details) is unanimous. John is the baptizer and the forerunner. His baptism prepares men's hearts to receive the message of Jesus, and is indeed an essential stage in the calling and mission of Jesus himself. His appearance on the stage of history is understood as a sign of the dawning of that new age which is to burst upon mankind through the work and teaching of Jesus. But none of this, as we shall see, is of importance to the author of the Fourth Gospel. His answer to the question about John the Baptist is a different one. John came 'to bear witness to Jesus'.

We should expect, then, that John the Baptist would make his appearance (and make it, in this Gospel, as a 'witness') at the beginning of the story. But our problem is to see a connection between this appearance and the opening verses of the Johannine prologue. Before tackling this, we must make a second preliminary point, this time about 'witnesses' in general. To be satisfied of the truth of a proposition, the western mind, conditioned by centuries of inductive reasoning, requires verifiable evidence. We feel instinctively that any statement we are required to believe must be capable of proof. If a man appears claiming to be the rightful heir to an estate, we demand that he should produce satisfactory evidence to substantiate his claim. But to the Jewish mind (and the Jews were by no means alone in this in the ancient world) the matter was seen differently. The question was not so much, How can he prove it? as, Whose word can we trust? If a citizen who enjoyed the respect of society solemnly affirmed that something was the case, this was all one could ask for. If two or three such citizens gave identical evidence (and stood up to cross-examination), this was sufficient even to condemn a man to death. There was no need to look further into the *facts*. The all-important question was the character of the witnesses.[3]

A vivid example of how this might work out in practice

---

[3] Even the systematic examination and cross-examination of witnesses was unknown before the Talmudic period. cf. H. E. Goldin, *Hebrew Criminal Law and Procedure* (1952), 157.

can be found among the Daniel stories in the Apocrypha.[4] Susanna had been unjustly accused of adultery with a fictitious lover by the two elders who had tried to seduce her. They gave their evidence; and the narrator goes on, 'As they were elders of the people and judges, the assembly believed them and condemned her to death' (Daniel and Susanna 41). That is to say, the 'court' was not required to consider the plausibility of the elders' story, but only the degree to which their character and status made them people whose evidence could be trusted. Had it not been for Daniel's intervention, the death sentence would have been carried out simply on the strength of their testimony. But it is equally instructive to observe how their evidence was overturned. A modern tale would doubtless have introduced a new piece of evidence which would have brought about a last minute reprieve. But Daniel had no new facts at his disposal. He was not a witness of the alleged crime. He had only a hunch about the true character of the witnesses. Even so, he could hardly have challenged them had he not held a special place in the people's esteem; and this is recognized in the text which runs: 'The rest of the elders said to him, "Come, take your place among us and state your case, for God has given you the standing of an elder"' (50). Even then, Daniel does not offer an alternative explanation of the facts, or present any new evidence; he merely subjects the two elders to independent examination and succeeds in discrediting them as reliable witnesses. No one asks what really happened (this is known only to the reader). It is sufficient to have shown that the original evidence must have been false; and the elders are then punished, not for their attempted adultery, but for what was regarded as an equally serious matter: giving false evidence on a capital charge.

[4] The view (proposed by N. Brüll in 1877 and taken up by, e.g., W. O. E. Oesterley, *An Introduction to the Books of the Apocrypha* (1935), 283–5) that the story was written in the climate of a move to amend the law of evidence has not been universally accepted. cf. R. H. Pfeiffer, *History of New Testament Times*, 451–2. This question does not greatly affect the value of the story as an illustration of fundamental attitudes.

In the light of this instinctive concern for the reliability of
the witnesses who can be called in support of any claim, we
shall be less surprised by the early appearance, in a Gospel
of which the express purpose is to persuade men to 'believe'
(20.31), of one whom the first Christians will have regarded
as a particularly dependable witness, John the Baptist. We
may now return to the opening verses of the prologue and
the problem posed by the apparently abrupt introduction of
the Baptist. Jesus, this writer would have us understand, was
not merely the Messiah of Jewish expectation: he was the
logos, a principle of the universe itself: 'Through him all
things came to be.' Moreover, it was through knowledge of
him that mankind could come truly to live: 'In him was life,
and that life was the light of men.' Then comes the first statement of the fundamental paradox which underlies any and
every gospel: 'The light shines in the darkness, but the darkness did not understand (or overcome) it.' How is the reader
to think of the 'light' and the 'darkness' which are personified
in these verses? They are not merely poetic symbols. Rather
they are to be imagined as adversaries in the heavenly court.
Jesus is the 'light'. But his claim to be so is not accepted by
his adversary, 'darkness'. And darkness, the prologue goes on
to show, includes the whole world, it includes even 'his own'.
That is to say (if we may now present the matter in a less
mythological way), the reader of the Gospel must face the
fact that virtually the whole world has continued to pass judgement against Jesus. If Jesus could be described as 'light' (and
the Gospel will later suggest that Jesus did so describe himself), then it was appropriate to describe all those who failed
to accept him as 'darkness'.[5] In order, then, that it may be
clear from the outset that the trial is still on, that the case
of Jesus can still be mounted, the reader must be told right
at the start that Jesus was not totally unrecognized. There

---

[5] The conception of the adversaries of God being 'children' (or
'captives') of darkness goes back to at least Wisd. 17—18, and is
familiar from the Dead Sea Scrolls. It is implied also by Matt. 5.14;
Luke 8.16. It is a short step from this to calling them 'darkness' itself.

were witnesses who could be called to support his claims. And the greatest of these was John the Baptist. Here was a witness whose dependability was taken for granted in Christian circles, and who had the additional authenticity of one who was deemed to have been foretold in the Old Testament. He is therefore introduced, in an appropriate scriptural idiom,[6] without further delay: 'There was a man sent from God whose name was John.'

John the Baptist, then, is the first witness in the case. When he next appears (1.15) we are given a fragment of his evidence. That it *is* evidence, rather than (say) proclamation or prophecy, is very heavily emphasized. Not only does the sentence begin, 'John gives evidence (*martyrei*) about him'; but it continues with a concrete example of this evidence, announced by a verb which in this Gospel seems always to draw attention to a highly significant utterance, and may indeed have a meaning particularly appropriate to the voice of a witness,[7] 'He cried

[6] For an analysis of the semitisms in this verse, see R. Bultmann, *The Gospel of John* (ET 1971), 48, n.3. Luke, after his own highly sophisticated introduction, falls into a similar scriptural style (1.5): ἐγένετο ἐν ταῖς ἡμέραις Ἡρῴδου βασιλέως κτλ.

[7] C. H. Dodd, *Interpretation*, 382, n.1, argues that 'John used κράζειν when most other Christian writers used κηρύσσειν, and in the same sense'. But the context here is μαρτυρία: κηρύσσειν would be quite inappropriate. κράζειν is used in classical Greek in connection with μαρτυρεῖν: cf. Dem. *De Cor.* 132; 199 διεμαρτύρου ... κεκραγώς; Plut. *Cat.Min.* 58 (1 787d) μαρτυρόμενος καὶ κεκραγὼς ἐν τῷ συνεδρίῳ. More significantly still, the word appears several times in a petition (P.Ox. 717, late first century B.C.) in what appears to be a forensic context, once with ἐν τῷ συνεδρίῳ. Perhaps this is the clue to another papyrus fragment (P.Ox. 2353, A.D. 32) which baffled its first editor: κραζόμενα φάσκεις καὶ ἐγὼ φάσκω, 'you are appealing to attested facts and so am I'. It is also possible that the strange phrase in Ignatius, τρία μυστήρια κραυγῆς, has an explanation along these lines (rather than those suggested by D. Daube, *JTS* 16 (1965), 128–9): 'Three mysteries, nevertheless made known by solemn testimony'. At any rate, the forensic sense certainly reappears in the New Testament at Rom. 8.15, πνεῦμα υἱοθεσίας, ἐν ᾧ κράζομεν ... συμμαρτυρεῖ (cf. Gal. 4.6); Acts 23.6, ἔκραζεν ἐν τῷ συνεδρίῳ. The 'shouting' (ἔκραζον) of the demons in Mark 3.11 is also, as we shall see, evidential.

aloud' (*kekrāgen*). Again, a few sentences later, we are explicitly told that 'this is the evidence of John' (1.19), and the striking phrase with which John answers the deputation from Jerusalem also has the ring of the law court:[8] 'He affirmed (*homologēsen*), and did not deny, but affirmed ...' (1.20). We must refer to the content of this evidence later. Meanwhile, it is important to notice the formal structure of the scenes which follow. This structure is threefold; and again, once the importance of these scenes as evidence is grasped, a logical progression emerges. The Baptist has already referred to his evidence about 'one who was to come'. In the first stage of his evidence, the question he is asked by the Jews is (characteristically, for this Gospel) the wrong question. They ask him about himself; whereas the real question to be asked is about Jesus. John's evidence, at this stage, consists of a series of disclaimers about his own status, and then a statement that somewhere, unknown to all, stands the person to whom his evidence refers: 'Among you, though you do not know him, stands the one who is to come after me' (1.26). At this stage, that is to say, his evidence is confident, but not precise: such a person certainly exists, but his whereabouts and identity are not known. The next stage requires a change of scene, most conveniently effected by the passage of time ('on the next day', 1.29). This time Jesus is present and John can actually point to him. No longer, Such a person exists, but, This is the person I was talking about (1.30). The evidence has become direct and ostensive. Finally (and a new stage is again marked by the passage of a day, 1.35) the evidence is accepted and corroborated by others. John did not speak his evidence in vain: by certain persons his word was accepted on the strength of the credibility of him who offered it. His role is well summed up later in the Gospel: 'John did no miraculous sign, but all that John said about this man was true' (10.42).

It is unnecessary to continue this analysis through chapter

---

[8] R. Bultmann, *The Gospel of John* (ET 1971), 88, n.1, to which add the papyrus evidence assembled in Moulton and Milligan, *Vocabulary of the Greek Testament* s.v. ὁμολογεῖν.

3 (to which in any case we must return in a moment) and through the few remaining passages in the Fourth Gospel which make reference to John the Baptist. Sufficient has already been said to warrant two important conclusions: first, that the initial appearance of John the Baptist in this Gospel, and the first statements he makes, allow him to appear consistently and exclusively as a *witness*; and secondly, that when the function and importance of such a witness in a Jewish milieu is rightly understood, some of those passages which appear at first sight to indicate disorderly and haphazard compilation in the Gospel as we have it can be seen as logical developments in the thought of an author who well understood what he was doing. But the question then arises: how does this presentation of John the Baptist square with that in the Synoptic Gospels?

The short answer to this question is that it does not square at all. Nowhere in the Synoptic Gospels is the Baptist referred to as a 'witness', and no saying of his is explicitly cited as 'evidence'. Yet the contrast must not be overdrawn; the difference may be not so much one of fact as of interpretation. Consider, for example, one of the basic components of the tradition about John the Baptist which occurs in all the Gospels: 'A voice crying in the wilderness: make straight the way of the Lord'. That this verse of Isaiah had been fulfilled in the person of John the Baptist may be said to have been a common conviction among Christians from the very earliest times. The quotation is the starting-point from which the Gospels of Mark and Matthew introduce John the Baptist; and it has a prominent place also in Luke and John. This, then, was clearly a piece of tradition held in common by all the Gospel writers, and one out of which (to put it rather crudely) they had to make what they could. What, they had to ask themselves, was the meaning of this 'voice' and its message? Up to a point, the riddle was not too difficult. The passage fitted admirably one whose activity was indeed situated in the wilderness and whose work seemed to be essentially preparatory—a preparation for something greater to follow.

But this could hardly be the whole answer: there must surely
be a deeper meaning than this. We now know, for example,
that the community responsible for the Dead Sea Scrolls also
saw its role as ultimately fulfilling this same prophecy: the
study of the Law, conducted in the desert, far from the con-
taminating influence of Jerusalem, was the necessary preparation (they believed) for the new age.[9] To Christians—and
doubtless to himself and his own followers—John the Baptist
was clearly a more precise, a less ambiguous, fulfilment of the
Isaiah prophecy than this. Now the way in which any instructed
reader instinctively probed deeper into the meaning of such a
text was by finding another which shared some of its language
and so could be used to cast new light upon it. The new text
chosen was from Malachi (3.1): 'Behold, I send my messenger
to prepare my way before me.'[10] This had sufficient verbal
contacts with the Isaiah passage for it to be reasonable to suppose that it alluded to the same thing. By itself, it did not add
very much. But it had become customary to interpret this
passage, in turn, in the light of the closing verses of Malachi
which explicitly mention Elijah. And so the original Isaiah
passage turned out to contain the key to the identity of John
the Baptist: he was Elijah—a conclusion underlined in Mark's
Gospel by the details of his description of the Baptist (which
includes several traits traditionally associated with Elijah) and
confirmed in Matthew's Gospel by a saying attributed to Jesus
himself ('If you will receive it, he is Elijah who is to come'—
11.14). Only in Luke, perhaps, out of the three Synoptic Gospels, is there any hesitation about this identification.

This identification was exciting and attractive. It clarified
at once the relationship between John and Jesus: John was
that Elijah who, it was believed, must certainly come before,
but only just before, the messianic age began. But it also
brought with it considerable difficulties. For how could a figure

---

[9] I QS. viii. 12–16.
[10] This is quoted, in a different context, by both Matthew and
Luke; in Mark it is actually conflated with the quotation from Isaiah
with which the Gospel opens.

who suffered the fate of John the Baptist possibly be a glorious Elijah *redivivus*? This was similar to the question about Jesus: how could this humble and suffering man possibly be the Messiah? And an answer was sought along the same lines: a passage of Scripture must be found—however difficult in the case of Elijah[11]—which predicted Elijah's sufferings. The question forms the topic of some sayings of Jesus in Matthew (17.12–13). Thus the identification of John with Elijah, starting from the traditional association of John with the prophecy about the Voice in Isaiah 40.3, may well have generated, or at least caused the preservation of, the discussion about John's nature and mission which we find in the Synoptic Gospels.

In the Fourth Gospel the matter is quite different. Isaiah 40.3 is indeed quoted; but there is no hint anywhere in the Gospel that it is to be interpreted in the light of Malachi, or that John the Baptist is to be identified with Elijah.[12] On the contrary, when John is asked by the priests and levites from Jerusalem whether he is Elijah, his answer is emphatically No. In other words, the author of this Gospel does not appear to follow the lead set by the Synoptics in using the Isaiah prophecy as an occult clue to the real identity of John the Baptist.[13]

---

[11] The citation of the γραφή in Mark 9.13 remains something of a mystery. The date of an apocryphal Jewish scripture on Elijah's sufferings (Jeremias in *TWNT* II, 942f, ET 940f) is still uncertain. cf. W. Wink, *John the Baptist in the Gospel Tradition* (1968), 14, n.2.

[12] Though some of the language used about John—particularly in John 5.35—seems to derive from traditional descriptions of Elijah (cf. Dodd, 266), just as some of the language used about Jesus does, particularly in Luke's Gospel.

[13] Dodd (*HTFG*, 266) suggests that at this point 'the Fourth Gospel ... appears to reflect a stage at which this assimilation [of John with Elijah] had not completely taken place'. But it is possible also that the author was exercising his own imagination (as perhaps the other evangelists, or the sources they used, did) to discover the true significance of Isaiah's prophecy as applied to the Baptist.

Indeed his solution was along different lines altogether. Instead of regarding the text as a prophecy *about* John the Baptist—in other words, as a cryptic description of him—he reported it as a saying *by* John the Baptist. John has just refused any of the titles—Christ, Elijah, prophet—suggested by his Jewish questioners. When pressed to say something positive about himself, he replies, 'I am the voice of one crying in the wilderness, "Make straight the way of the Lord" ' (RSV). So that is what he is: a voice. And this, for the fourth evangelist, is sufficient.[14] It is as a voice, a speaker giving evidence, that John is important. There is no need to ask those further questions about his identity which cause such confusion in the other Gospels. It is simply as a witness that this writer wishes John the Baptist to be understood and remembered.

To this extent, the difference between the Fourth Gospel and the Synoptics in their treatment of John the Baptist may be regarded as no more than a difference of interpretation of the same historical material. But there is one discrepancy between them which does seem to involve a question of fact. In the Fourth Gospel John the Baptist is seen primarily, and almost exclusively, as a witness, whereas on one occasion in Matthew and Luke he is reported to have been quite uncertain about Jesus' Messiahship—to have been, in fact, precisely the opposite of a confident and reliable witness. This discrepancy is a real one. It cannot be explained away,[15] and we are forced to choose. We must ask whether the episode recorded in Matthew and Luke really has the strength to overturn the whole presentation of John the Baptist as a witness which dominates the early chapters of the Fourth Gospel.

[14] This distinction is well stated by B. Lindars, *New Testament Apologetic* (1961), 206, n.5: 'The use of Isa. 40.3 is to define the Baptist's *function* .... note that John 1.23 accurately represents this functional motive.... It has come into the synoptic tradition in contexts concerned with the Baptist's *identity*. ...'

[15] Attempts to do so are artificial, cf. Dodd, *HTFG*, 296.

In Matthew, the passage runs as follows:

'John, who was in prison, heard what Christ was doing, and
sent his own disciples to him with this message: "Are you
the one who is to come, or are we to expect some other?"
Jesus answered, "Go and tell John what you hear and see:
the blind recover their sight, the lame walk, the lepers are
made clean, the deaf hear, the dead are raised to life, the poor
are hearing the good news—and happy is the man who does
not find me a stumbling-block"' (11.2–6).

The kernel of this passage is evidently a saying of Jesus which
proclaims the fulfilment of those scriptural prophecies which
foretold and described a new age to come. The form of this
saying is significant. Jesus does not say, 'I have been curing
the blind and the lame ... therefore I am indeed the one who
was to come.' Rather he draws attention to certain things
which are going on; by describing them in the terms of Old
Testament prophecies he implies that they are signs of the
new age. If the new age has come, then there must be a person
whose appearance has brought it into being. This person, of
course, is Jesus; but Jesus is so unlike what people expected
the Coming One to be that they could easily be put off (the
actual word is 'scandalized').[16] However, the important thing
—and this is the whole emphasis of the saying—is to discern
the signs of the times, to recognize the dawning of the new
age. The identification of Jesus as the key person in that new
age is a necessary sequel, but it comes later. It is by no means
the first thing to be attended to.

This saying has the ring of authenticity. It is in harmony
with the veiled way in which Jesus so often speaks of his own
role in the bringing about of God's kingdom; it is in harmony
also with the concept of the messianic age as it was held in
the time of Jesus and as it is still held in Judaism today—
namely, that the important question is always whether or not
the new age has begun; identifying the Messiah is a secondary

---

[16] ὃς ἐὰν μὴ σκανδαλίσθη ἐν ἐμοί.

task.[17] But if the saying itself is authentic, its context, and in particular the question which leads up to it, can hardly be so. For the question does not fit the answer. We have seen that the answer directs attention first to the state of the world, and only then allows a glance at the person of Jesus. But the question is all about Jesus: are you he that should come? Luke, when writing up the same episode, seems to have seen the difficulty (7.18–23). He says that 'at that moment Jesus cured many of their diseases,' and so forth. In other words, he succeeds in making Jesus' reply look like a direct reference to his own miracles, so that it becomes a more appropriate answer to the question. But this is clearly artificial. The fact remains that the question does not really fit the answer; and along with the majority of modern commentators we must follow the form critics and regard the episode as one that was invented to provide a setting for a well-remembered saying of Jesus. The invention was not entirely successful, and in any case fails to reckon with that understanding of John the Baptist as a witness which was so firmly grasped by the author of the Fourth Gospel. But it certainly need not now be regarded as a piece of historical information secure enough to throw doubt upon that whole concept.

Thus the Fourth Gospel's presentation of the Baptist as primarily a witness must be allowed to stand alongside, and to supplement, the synoptic presentation of him as herald and forerunner. In conclusion, we must ask whether this understanding of the Baptist was an original insight of the fourth evangelist—and therefore to be regarded as no more than a secondary interpretation of the primary facts contained in the other Gospels—or whether it was already present much earlier in the tradition, in which case the fourth evangelist must take the credit for having rescued it and restored to it its original significance. An answer to this question is suggested by one passage in the synoptic tradition which we have not yet brought into the discussion (Mark 11.27–33; Matt. 21.23–7; Luke 20.1–8).

[17] See above, p. 9.

The passage occurs in all the Synoptic Gospels, and the only variations in the three accounts are easily explicable on stylistic grounds. It describes how the Jewish teachers asked Jesus by what authority he did these things, and how Jesus retaliated by asking them what authority they ascribed to John the Baptist. This is, once again, a passage with the ring of authenticity. Jesus' counter-question is well in the rabbinic tradition of discussion, yet it has a brilliance and aptness which can only be original—and indeed commentators are almost unanimous in regarding it as an unimpeachable utterance of Jesus.[18] In the verses that follow, however, the hand of the narrator is discernible. 'They discussed among themselves, saying, if we say from heaven, he will say, why then did you not believe him?' What the lawyers and elders said among themselves is hardly likely to have been remembered *verbatim*; but it was essential for the evangelist to show why Jesus' counter-question put his interlocutors in such a difficult position. What is striking is the way the evangelist did so. The point at issue was that of authority: by what authority—*exousia*—had Jesus been doing what he had been doing?[19] This is a surprisingly Johannine question. Indeed it is answered in John's Gospel far more explicitly than it is in the Synoptics: 'The father has given him authority—*exousia*—to pass judgement, because he is Son of Man' (5.27). Moreover, the question of Jesus' authority to do and say what he does is at the centre of a number of controversies in John's Gospel. In particular, the passage just quoted goes on to link this question of Jesus' authority with the validity of the evidence which he can adduce to support his claims. In other words, to ask 'by what authority' is equivalent to asking, 'what

[18] cf. V. Taylor, *The Gospel, according to Mark* ad loc.: 'It is excessive scientific caution to ask whether 28–30 is an historical account or a formation of the community.'

[19] It is open to question whether ταῦτα in v.28 refers to the cleansing of the temple or to Jesus' work in general (cf. Vincent Taylor ad loc.). This ambiguity may be a sign that the pericope has lost its original context (Bultmann, *History of the Synoptic Tradition* (ET 1963), 19f). But none of this affects the point at issue.

grounds are there for believing you to be someone entitled to speak and act in this way; what are your credentials?' And a verse or two later Jesus is made to say, 'You sent to John, and he has given evidence for the truth' (5.33). The whole question of Jesus' authority, in John's Gospel, is closely linked with that of his credentials, of the evidence he can produce. And on this question, the evidence of John the Baptist was highly significant.

The Synoptic Gospels do not pursue the question in these terms; yet if we look at the passage in question, there is one detail which shows a startling affinity to Johannine thinking. The lawyers and elders are made to say, 'If we say that John's baptism was from heaven, he will say, why then did you not....'—and we expect a verb like 'accept it', or even, 'why did you not repent?'. But what Mark has written is, 'Why did you not believe him?' Elsewhere in the synoptic accounts, the appropriate response to John the Baptist is always to repent, to be baptized, and to undergo a moral conversion in the face of the coming crisis. But here, Mark acknowledges that the appropriate response is 'to believe him'. And who is the person whom it is important to believe? Why, the man who gives evidence, the witness—which is, of course, exactly how John's Gospel presents the Baptist. Here then, at least, is an indication that Mark was aware of John as a person whose significance lay in the evidence he gave. In which case, we need no longer say that the Johannine picture of John is individual and eccentric: it was one known also to Mark, even though he and those who followed him chose in the main to concentrate on other aspects of the Baptist's significance. It may well be correct to understand John as the forerunner of Jesus (as the Synoptics suggest); but it is equally legitimate to follow the interpretation offered by the Fourth Gospel and understand him as the first and greatest witness to the proposition that Jesus is the Christ. Moreover, the evidence of the Baptist was weighty. He was 'a man sent from God'—that is, his claim to know truth about God was a strong one; and in fact (according to the Fourth Gospel) he was able to appeal to

God as the source of his information (1.33), just as Jesus was
to do later in the story. And his evidence culminated in a
statement of great significance and utter finality, 'This is the
Son of God'. The purpose of the whole Gospel is summed up
in 20.31, 'so that you should believe that Jesus is the Christ,
the Son of God'. The reader who is to be persuaded of the
truth of this amazing proposition will have been much influenced by the fact that these are exactly the words that were
used by the most authoritative of all human witnesses to Jesus:
John the Baptist.

OTHER WITNESSES

But John the Baptist was not the only witness who could be
appealed to. The first Christian disciples were also men who
presumably recognized Jesus for what he was, and whose evidence could be trusted, since they had become the actual
founders of the Church. And so, when the fourth evangelist
introduces these first disciples of Jesus, he does so as a direct
sequel to his presentation of John the Baptist. Their evidence
complements his evidence. They, like him, were witnesses.
And it is important to show that they were the kind of witnesses
who were to be trusted, that they had good reasons on which
to base their evidence. This concern determines the presentation in this Gospel of Jesus' call to the first disciples, and
makes the narrative read somewhat differently from that in
the other Gospels.

The passage which concerns us begins at 1.35. A day has
passed since John the Baptist gave his own decisive testimony
to Jesus, and the scene is set for what we have called the
third phase of John's witness, the phase in which his evidence
comes to be accepted by others. John the Baptist repeats, in
the presence of two of his own disciples, his acclamation of
Jesus as 'the lamb of God' (1.36). 'The two disciples heard
him say this, and followed Jesus' (1.37). This represents an
interesting departure from the normal pattern of call and
response as it occurs in the other Gospels. There, Jesus simply
summons men to follow, and they respond immediately. No

explanation is given; and only Luke seems to have been aware of the psychological question raised by this procedure, for it is he who has inserted the story of the miraculous draft of fishes to explain why Peter immediately left his trade to follow Jesus (5.1–11). But in John's Gospel the motives of all the first disciples are fully explained. Andrew and another follower of John the Baptist hear John's testimony, and since they are disciples—literally 'learners', *talmidim*—of John, they have no choice but to accept it and act upon it. They then start a kind of chain reaction. Andrew gives his evidence to his brother Simon, who, being his brother, is disposed to accept it. This makes two disciples from Bethsaida. Jesus then meets Philip, and commands him (in a manner typical of the call narratives in the Synoptics) to follow him. Philip immediately responds; but again this Gospel offers an explanation. Philip also came from Bethsaida, and so knew personally the standing of Andrew and Simon: he knew that he could accept their evidence.[20]

So far, then, the evidence has been accepted by four men, each of whom heard it from a source he was disposed to trust. But the appearance of Nathanael introduces a new factor. Nathanael (so far as we are told) has no particular reason to believe what Philip tells him: he is neither a kinsman nor a close neighbour. And in fact he refuses to accept his evidence, on the grounds that it conflicts with all that he has known up to now about Galileans ('Can anything good come from Nazareth?'—1.46). He has to be brought to Jesus before he is convinced.

In studying the Nathanael episode, it is necessary to understand the tasks which lay before the writer. On the one hand he had to explain why Nathanael came to recognize Jesus for what he was; and on the other he had to give reasons to his Christian readers for attaching importance to the testimony which Nathanael gave—for Nathanael was not remembered as one of the Twelve, and had no fixed place in the list of

---

[20] John is fond of such explanations; cf. 12.9; 18.2.

Christian witnesses.[21] Something needed therefore to be said about him which would commend him as one whose word was to be trusted. The first point was met easily enough. Jesus, by telling Nathanael exactly where he had just been (sitting under a fig-tree) showed that he possessed telepathic powers; and this was sufficient to mark him out as an exceptional person —it elicited the confession from Nathanael, 'You are the Son of God, you are the King of Israel' (1.49), just as a similar feat of psychic perception elicited from the woman of Samaria the confession 'You are a prophet' (4.19), and was a factor in the people of Samaria's confession, '[You are] the Saviour of the world' (4.42). But this statement of Nathanael's expressed (like John the Baptist's confession in 1.34) exactly the proposition which the whole Gospel set out to prove (20.31), that Jesus is the Christ, the Son of God. It was essential, therefore, to meet the second of the points just mentioned, and to show why the readers of the Gospel should give weight to the evidence of one, Nathanael, who had gained no clear status in the Christian movement.

This second point is met in a rather more subtle way. Jesus (again exercising psychic powers) says to Nathanael, 'Here is a true Israelite, in whom there is no guile.' Each half of this statement is important. Note first that Nathanael is called, not a Jew, but an Israelite. In John's Gospel, 'the Jews' are normally Jesus' opponents, men who signally fail to recognize him and give correct evidence about him; and had Nathanael been one of these, his study of the Torah would have led him to no better conclusions than those reached by Jesus' learned enemies. But no, he is called an Israelite, that is, an inheritor of the promises made by God to his own people, but not a party to the 'Jewish' antagonism to the truth as re-

[21] There is no convincing way of harmonizing the appearance of Nathanael here with the lists of the Twelve elsewhere, nor is there any hint in the text that Nathanael became one of the regular disciples. The mention of him at 21.2 proves nothing. The entire case for Nathanael's admissibility as a witness must rest on this passage alone.

vealed in Jesus.[22] Secondly, Nathanael is without guile—and
this, of course, is precisely what is required of a reliable witness.[23] Thus, with great economy and subtlety, the writer
builds up the authority of Nathanael as a witness; and having
done so, he allows Nathanael to give his evidence, the last in
the whole series of testimonies: 'Rabbi, you are the Son of
God, you are king of Israel' (1.49).[24]

There is no further occasion in John's Gospel on which a
disciple is explicitly called upon to give evidence about Jesus.
But there is one scene where the theme is implicit. At the end
of Jesus' long discourse about heavenly bread in chapter 6,
some of the disciples dissociate themselves from him; where-
upon Jesus turns to the Twelve and says, 'Do you also want
to leave me?' (6.67). Simon Peter replies (clearly speaking on
behalf of the Twelve) 'Lord, to whom shall we go? Your words
are words of eternal life.' This last phrase is distinctively
Johannine; but there is a phrase in the next sentence which is
unique in this Gospel: 'We have believed and have known
that you are *the holy one of God.*' This is clearly a very important affirmation about Jesus.[25] We must examine, first its
formal context, and then its content.

It is not said that Simon Peter offers this statement as
evidence.[26] Yet the form of his statement is reminiscent of the
evidence of John the Baptist, who, as we have seen, frequently
quotes statements he has made in the past ('I saw, and gave

[22] There are literary antecedents to this distinction between
Ἰσραηλίτης and Ἰουδαῖος. See *TWNT* III, 361–6, ET III, 359–65.
[23] ἄδολος, cf. Proverbs 12.17, LXX ὁ δὲ μάρτυς τῶν ἀδίκων δόλιος.
[24] This by no means exhausts the possibilities of the Nathanael
episode. cf. J. D. M. Derrett in *Heythrop Journal* 14 (1973), 261–4
(who convincingly suggests a midrashic treatment of Zech. 3.8–10);
and K. Berger, *NTS* 20 (1973), 5, n.19: 'knowing the thoughts of
men' was a standard accomplishment of the ideal King, as in
Wisd. 7.20.
[25] It was recognized as such by early copyists, who conflated it
with other christological titles and produced a mass of variant
readings.
[26] The words μαρτυρεῖν or μαρτυρία do not appear.

my evidence ...'—1.34, etc.). Peter does not say, 'We believe you are the Christ' but 'We have believed and known that you are the Christ.' That is to say, he is not offering merely the subjective belief of the disciples; he is alluding to an objective occasion in the past when they not only attained their conviction, but in fact received evidence so compelling that they were able to say 'We know'. In other words, though he and the rest of the Twelve are not at this moment being called upon to give evidence about Jesus (since they are talking privately with him), they are showing their readiness to do so should the occasion arise. The reader is expected to note their affirmation as one more piece of evidence about Jesus.

This understanding of the verse both illuminates and is confirmed by an otherwise puzzling feature of Jesus' reply. 'Did I not choose you, the twelve? And one of you is a devil—meaning Judas Iscariot' (6.70–1, RSV). This is the usual translation of *diabolos*, but it is one which has no parallel, either in the New Testament, or in Jewish literature. *Diabolos*, slanderer, is a name for the devil himself, for Satan. The devil's underlings are demons; there is no instance of *diabolos* being used of any but the prince of evil himself. Therefore the only legitimate translation of it here would be 'One of you is the devil'. This would not give an impossible sense. Jesus could presumably call Judas 'the devil' just as, on one occasion, he calls Peter 'Satan'. Yet, in this context, actually to identify Judas with the devil does not seem particularly appropriate; moreover, on two occasions in chapter 13 the writer actually distinguishes between Judas and the devil ('the devil having put it into his heart to betray Jesus'—13.2; 'then Satan entered into him'—13.27). As an alternative, let us consider a different rendering altogether: 'one of you is a slanderer, an adversary'. The disciples have just demonstrated what their evidence would be. Jesus accepts this, but points out that one of them will give his evidence on the other side, as a *diabolos*. This is, of course, a biblical and perhaps rather literary conception (but not for that reason improbable in John's Gospel). The role of the *diabolos* is exactly defined in

Psalm 108.6, LXX, 'Let his adversary stand on his right hand', and still more clearly in Zechariah 3.1, 'His adversary stood on his right hand to oppose him'. The context in each of these passages is that of a court hearing, and the slanderer, or adversary, may even be standing in the position denoting greatest trust, that is, on the right hand side of the defendant. But it may be asked, is Judas actually cast in this role of *diabolos*? Not in so many words. But when, at the critical moment of his treachery, Jesus is found in Gethsemane by the party sent to arrest him, the writer records that 'Judas who betrayed him stood with them' (18.5). This statement adds nothing to the action. We already know that Judas was there; and that he should simply have been 'standing' seems at first sight unexpected. But in each of the Old Testament passages quoted, the adversary 'stands' in the court. Here Judas, by 'standing' with Jesus' enemies, identifies himself again as *diabolos*.

There are hints, then, in the formal context of this statement about Jesus that it is intended to be understood as a further piece of evidence, vouched for by the Twelve (though one of them, Judas, subsequently turned his coat and gave evidence *against* Jesus), and therefore to be weighed very seriously by Christian readers. We must now turn to the content. 'You are the holy one of God.' This is arresting. The phrase occurs nowhere else in John's Gospel, and in only one other place in the New Testament (Mark 1.24). For the title, 'the holy one of God', there is no precedent in the Old Testament,[27] nor in Hellenistic or Palestinian Judaism. Nor, in any case, is it a sound approach to seek some sect or environment where this title may have been in use, since there is no reason why either the disciples or the early Christian writers should have 'borrowed' it from such a source. It is better to recognize

[27] E. Schweizer, *The Good News according to Mark* (ET 1971), 52, draws attention to the fact that, in Judg. 13.7 and 16.17, LXX (B) reads ἅγιος θεοῦ instead of (A) ναζιραῖος. But in these passages the phrase is essentially adjectival, and does not express the unique status which is implied by the occurrences in the New Testament.

that this is one of that very small class of Jesus' titles which
were *new* when they were first applied to him, and were intended to express his identity, not in terms of some traditional
figure (such as Messiah) but as something unprecedented and
unique—not 'a holy man' (of which there had been many
before) but '*the* holy man of God', not 'a son of God' (which
was something which could be said, in some sense, of a number
of people) but '*the* son of God' (which, so far as we know,[28]
had not been said, and indeed could not be said, of anybody).
The meaning of such titles has to be found, not in their alleged
usage elsewhere, but in the significance attached to them by
the first Christians who acknowledged them.

There are several reasons for seeing some connection[29]
between 'the holy one of God' and 'the Son of God'.

i   'The holy one of God', in Mark 1.24, is the title given to
    Jesus by a demon (and it must be remembered that
    demons had access to knowledge about Jesus, so that their
    evidence was very significant). The only other title given
    to him by demons (and again this is important as evi-
    dence) is 'the Son of God' (Mark 3.11; 5.7). Clearly both
    these titles express a highly significant fact about Jesus,
    a fact which the demons are specially qualified to know.

ii In the angel's speech to Mary, Luke (1.35) includes the
    words 'the holy thing which is being born[30] shall be called

[28] For a recent judgement cf. E. Lohse in *TWNT* VIII, 361, 24–6,
ET VIII, 361: 'To date, no clear instance has been adduced to
support the view that in pre-Christian times Judaism used the title
"Son of God" for the Messiah.' This is disputed by F. Hahn,
The Titles of Jesus (ET 1969), 281–4, who sees indications in
B. Sukkah 52a (2nd century) and in some fragments from Qumran
that the title was already used of the Royal Messiah. This is a very
recondite origin for the title compared with that which we shall
advance later on.

[29] This connection is recognized by, e.g., O. Cullmann, *Christology
of the New Testament* (ET 1959), 285—'almost interchangeable'.

[30] καὶ τὸ γεννώμενον ἅγιον κληθήσεται υἱὸς θεοῦ. This is
grammatically a more probable translation that to take ἅγιον as
a predicate, parallel with υἱός. But for the present argument either
translation yields the same result.

the Son of God'. Luke is here writing poetically; but it is clear that it must have come naturally to him to associate the two expressions, 'holy' and 'Son', as descriptions of Jesus.

iii There are points of contact between the confession of Simon Peter in John's Gospel and the confession at Caesarea Philippi in the Synoptics.[31] In Mark and Luke, Peter confesses Jesus to be 'the Christ'. But in Matthew, this is expanded to 'the Christ, the Son of God' (Matt. 16.16). It does not of course follow that this is equivalent to 'the Holy one of God' in John;[32] but it does appear that both phrases were thought appropriate by the evangelists, or the traditions they were using, to express Peter's conviction of the uniqueness and greatness of Jesus.

None of these reasons is decisive on its own; but together they amount to a strong argument for the conclusion that, with the two expressions 'The Holy One of God' and 'The Son of God', we have to do with two formulas which were regarded by the evangelists as particularly significant statements about Jesus. On the basis, therefore, of content as well as form, we may regard Peter's statement in John 6.69, that Jesus is the Holy One of God, as belonging to the series of testimonies in which, first John the Baptist, and then Nathanael, acknowledge Jesus to be the Son of God (John 1.34; 1.49). And with this statement of Simon Peter (who, as we have seen, is here representing the Twelve) the series is brought to an end.

The resemblance between this passage in John's Gospel and the scene at Caesarea Philippi in Matthew's Gospel invites us to consider (as with the witness of John the Baptist) whether this theme of the disciples giving evidence about Jesus is distinctively (and perhaps originally) Johannine, or whether it also appears in the synoptic tradition. The superficial answer, again, is that the theme is peculiar to the Fourth Gospel: nowhere in the Synoptics are the disciples called 'witnesses',

[31] cf. Dodd, *HTFG*, 220.

[32] Though it may have seemed so to the copyists responsible for the Koine text of John 6.69, ὁ Χριστὸς ὁ υἱὸς τοῦ θεοῦ τοῦ ζῶντος.

nowhere do they make statements which can naturally be understood as 'evidence'. Yet to make this judgement without qualification is to ignore one very striking and consistent feature of all those passages in which Jesus is called Son of God. With only two exceptions (one of which is significant) these statements are *made by a heavenly being or on heavenly authority*. That is to say, if the reader is alert enough to receive them as evidence that Jesus is the Son of God (or the Holy One of God), the authority on which the evidence is given is exceedingly impressive.

It will be as well to spell out the point in detail. The occasions on which Jesus is addressed as, or described as, 'The Son of God' (or 'The Holy One of God') are as follows:

i   By the angel at his birth: 'the holy thing which is to be born shall be called the son of God' (Luke 1.35). Luke is of course writing freely here, and the passage has no weight as a piece of historical tradition. Yet it is significant that Luke (who was familiar with the Marcan tradition that other-worldly beings knew who Jesus was) should have put this phrase into the angel's mouth. The birth-stories in Matthew and Luke are both extended statements of the proposition that Jesus was, in a unique way, the Son of God; but in both the essential information (or evidence) is given on the authority of an angel.

ii   According to all three Synoptic Gospels, the voice from heaven which addresses Jesus at his baptism pronounces 'You are my son, my beloved'. Whatever Old Testament precedents there may be for this utterance (a question on which scholars are still divided) the essential fact is indisputable: Jesus is declared to be the Son of God by a heavenly voice.

iii   This testimony is repeated, in exactly the same terms, in all the synoptic accounts of the transfiguration, and is again uttered by a 'voice from the cloud' (Mark 9.7).

iv   In the temptation stories in Matthew and Luke, Satan introduces two of the three tests with the words, 'If you are the Son of God'. The logic of the episode demands that this is a real, not a hypothetical, condition. That is to say, Satan knows, and in this way declares, that Jesus *is* the Son of God.

v 'The demons shouted, You are the Son of God' (Mark 3.11). This well summarizes the way in which, on various occasions of exorcism by Jesus, the demons acclaim Jesus for what he is. Apart from the one variation (already noted) of 'The Holy one of God' (Mark 1.24), the only title by which the demons recognize Jesus is 'The Son of God' (Mark 5.7 and pars.). Jesus does not repudiate their acknowledgement of him; and their testimony (since they come from another world) is of great weight.

vi Matthew's account of Jesus stilling the storm (14.22–36) is the only one to include the episode of Peter's attempt to walk on the sea; and it ends (unlike Mark and John) with the sentence, 'Those in the boat worshipped him, saying, Truly you are the Son of God' (14.33). This acclamation, unlike the others, is an inference from miraculous events, not a piece of knowledge gained from heavenly sources. Scholars have pointed out[33] that this is the one instance of the title which recalls the Hellenistic sense of 'Son of God' meaning 'miracle-worker', and that it seems an unfortunate anticipation of the recognition of Jesus by Peter in 16.16. The occurrence is undoubtedly an anomaly in the sense we are considering; but it is probably better to accept it as such than to attempt to explain it away.[34]

vii In Matthew, again, the account of the recognition of Jesus by his disciples at Caesarea Philippi includes, not just the title 'The Christ', but also 'The Son of the living

[33] cf. Cullmann, *Christology of the New Testament*, 277, quoting J. Bieneck. Hahn, op. cit., 299–307, finds many more instances of the Hellenistic idea.

[34] Though explanations are not wanting, cf. H. J. Held in Bornkamm-Barth-Held, *Tradition and Interpretation in Matthew* (ET 1963), 266, 272: Matthew's writing up of the story is strongly influenced by the needs of a Hellenistic congregation.

God'. Jesus' response to this is highly significant: 'Flesh and blood has not revealed this to you, but my father who is in heaven.' Here, Peter's knowledge that Jesus is the Son of God is expressly attributed to a heavenly source. Peter's evidence has the greatest possible weight. In Matthew the episode is not only different from Mark and Luke in containing the formula 'Son of God': it also contains an essential indication that this (like all but one of the instances already considered) proceeds from a supernatural source.

viii The final instance is the significant exception. The Centurion, under the impact of Jesus' death, exclaims, 'Truly this man was the Son of God.' At this point, the question of the *source* of this witness's evidence is clearly irrelevant. What will influence the reader of the Gospel is that this testimony should have been elicited from a pagan.[35]

Of these eight instances, then, six are the utterances of beings from another world, or (in the case of Peter) of one whose knowledge proceeds from another world. This is a fact which demands explanation. Those who believe that 'Son of God' was a title which derived from the world of Hellenistic miracle-men have an explanation ready: the episodes in which Jesus was at work like such a miracle-man were precisely the episodes into which it was natural for the evangelists to import allegedly Hellenistic terminology such as 'Son of God'. This may in fact be the explanation of the one total exception listed above—the appearance of 'Son of God' in Matthew's account of the stilling of the storm (14.33).[36] But it does not account for the fact that otherwise it is only the exorcisms, out

[35] It is of course possible, with some scholars (e.g. Hahn, op. cit., 329, n.157) to see, in the centurion's confession, a typical instance of the death of a Hellenistic θεῖος ἀνήρ. But it is hard to believe, simply on the basis of a resemblance with other stories, that the incident carries so little significance. Moreover, if the words υἱοῦ θεοῦ are thought genuine in Mark 1.1, it is hard not to believe that the centurion's cry is recorded deliberately as an impressive endorsement of them.

[36] προσεκύνησαν is another such trait, noted by Held, loc. cit.

of all Jesus' miracles, which elicit this title, and that stress
seems to be laid on the other-worldly knowledge of those who
use it. A more likely explanation is that these acknowledge-
ments of Jesus as 'Son of God' or 'Holy One of God' are
recorded in the Synoptic Gospels precisely because they are
made (and normally are made only) by those who have access
to knowledge 'from above'. In the milieu in which they were
writing, it was not necessary for the evangelists to underline
the point. The importance of these utterances, and of the
authority on which they were made, as evidence about Jesus
will have been sufficiently obvious to their readers, even though
it has ceased to be obvious to us. These Gospels contain implicitly what we have seen to be explicit in the Fourth Gospel: a series of weighty testimonies to the proposition that
Jesus is the Son of God.

With this in mind, let us turn back for a moment to the
series of testimonies in John's Gospel. The first is that of
John the Baptist: 'I have seen and given evidence that this
is the Son of God' (1.34). But immediately before this, the
Baptist expressly mentions the source of his evidence: 'He
who sent me to baptize with water was the one who told
me . . .' (1.33). The reader need be in no doubt who is meant:
John was a man 'sent from God' (1.6). His evidence has the
authority of a message from God himself. The second piece
of evidence in the series is that of Nathanael: 'Rabbi, you are
the Son of God' (1.49). This time it is not said that Nathanael
had received a heavenly vision to authenticate his evidence—
this would have been impossible within the dramatic scheme
of the episode. Instead, Jesus expresses surprise that Nathanael
should believe this about him on relatively trivial grounds,
and promises him that he *will* have a heavenly vision to confirm the confession he has already made (1.50–1). Thirdly,
there is Peter's confession in 6.69. This again contains no
reference to a communication from another world. Yet the
way it is phrased ('We have believed and have known') points
to some experience in the past which would authenticate this
statement. The first readers of this Gospel may or may not

have picked up the hint. As we have seen, it is Matthew who makes the matter explicit: 'Flesh and blood did not reveal this to you, but my father who is in heaven' (16.17). But it is not altogether absent from Mark and Luke. For when (in these two Gospels) Peter shows himself unwilling to accept all that Jesus says about himself, he receives the rebuke 'You are considering, not the things of God, but the things of men' (Mark 8.33). In Mark, as in Matthew, Peter can give correct evidence only on the authority of a word from God, not on merely human authority.

We have now completed our review[37] of the witnesses whom this evangelist could call on to give their evidence to the reader that Jesus is Son of God and Messiah. We have seen that the credentials of these witnesses are carefully presented, and that there is more than a hint (though the matter is clearer in the Synoptics) that in each case their evidence was received on supernatural authority. At this point the action shifts to Jerusalem. The claims of Jesus are set against the judgement of 'the Jews'—that is to say, of those who represented the administration of the law of Moses, according to which law (as we saw at the beginning) this writer, like St Paul, acknowledges that Jesus was after due process found guilty. Before such judges, the witnesses called so far (with the exception of Nathanael and perhaps of John the Baptist—5.33–6) would have carried no weight: they had no pretensions to learning or influence. However impressive they might be to the Christian or even the non-Christian reader, they could hardly be introduced as a factor in any actual confrontation between Jesus and the Jews. From now on, the issue turned on other considerations. The case of Jesus, as presented before his contemporary judges, rested upon the word of one witness only: Jesus himself.

[37] We have left out of account the confession of Martha before the raising of Lazarus, 'I believe that you are the Christ, the Son of God' (11.27). A woman's testimony would not have been accepted in a court of law, and this is the one formulation of Jesus' true identity which seems to have no evidential function.

3

The Procedure

We must now glance again at Jewish legal procedure, which was in many ways startlingly different from our own. In the first place we must beware of the assumption (which we tend to make instinctively) that for a trial to take place at all it was necessary for the accused to appear before a formally constituted court. This was never the case in Old Testament times: justice was 'at the gate' of the city (Amos 5.15) and was administered by the 'elders', that is, the leading citizens in the place (Deut. 19.12), who might be called upon at any time (as in Ruth 4.1–12) to arrest an offender (Deut. 19.12), determine his guilt (Deut. 25.7–9), and either carry out the punishment themselves (Deut. 22.18–19) or command the witnesses of the deed to do so (Deut. 21.18–21). There were, of course, superior courts to which more difficult cases might be referred (Deut. 17.8–13): in biblical times these were staffed by priests or scribes, in later times they were organized in the form of local sanhedrins dependent upon the great Sanhedrin in Jerusalem. But despite the anxiety of the Pharisees to have all cases brought before regularly constituted courts, and despite the regulations which were later codified to govern the size and composition of courts necessary to deal with particular types of cases,[1] it is clear that the principle long remained in force that any three competent persons might be called upon at any time to hear a simple case and even to carry out the sentence.[2]

A second point of difference is that the distinction,

---

[1] M. Sanh. 1.

[2] On the normal procedures see J. D. M. Derrett, *NTS* 18 (1972), 180–1; id. *Law in the New Testament* (1970), 165. On procedure in the Old Testament, see L. Köhler, *Hebrew Man* (ET 1956), 149–72.

which we take for granted, between the function of a witness and the function of a judge was much less clear in the Jewish system than in modern western practice. We have already observed that a Jewish court was not much concerned (and indeed was not equipped) to investigate *facts*: the main question it had to decide was the admissibility and competence of the witnesses. In civil disputes this was primarily the concern of the litigants themselves, who could challenge the admissibility of each other's witnesses. The man with the more impressive array of witnesses normally won, and a single arbitrator could well be sufficient to settle the matter. In criminal cases there were further checks to be made: not only must the witnesses be reputable and respected people, but it must be clear to all that their testimony was not the result of collusion or corruption; therefore the presence of other respected persons, as 'judges', was essential.[3] But this virtually exhausted the function of these additional 'judges'. If the witnesses were found to be admissible and competent, and if their evidence was clear and unambiguous, conviction would follow automatically; and in many cases it was the same witnesses who would have the responsibility of carrying out the sentence.[4] Evidence, judgement, and sentence were thus much less clearly separated than would be conceivable in a western court.[5]

There is a third factor which must be taken into account if we are to understand fully the distinctive character of Jewish procedure. It could happen in certain cases that there might be only one witness.[6] Suppose, for example, that the deeds to a particular piece of ground had perished in the course of a war, and suppose that no witnesses could be produced to vouch for the person who claimed to be the legal inheritor. In such a case the claimant would be the only person with access to

[3] Derrett, op. cit., 165.

[4] Deut. 17.7; John 8.7.

[5] cf. Köhler, op. cit., 156–7, who concludes, 'judges and witnesses are therefore not differentiated'.

[6] A variety of such cases is envisaged in, e.g., M. Ketuboth 2.

knowledge of relevant evidence and the court would simply have to make up its mind whether to take his word for it. If he were a man enjoying great respect in society, it might be willing to do so. Alternatively, it might resort to an altogether different procedure: it might challenge the claimant to 'call God to witness', that is, to support his claim with an oath. If he were prepared to do this, a presumption would be created in favour of the truth of his statement. If it were false, God could be relied on (so it was believed) to punish him. But meanwhile the court had no business to doubt its truth. Indeed, if they did so, and if it turned out to be true (or if God clearly did not bring his own punishment on the man they suspected of being a perjurer), then they themselves would be in danger of incurring severe penalties.

This last point has an important bearing upon John's Gospel which will be considered later. But first, let us consider how this whole system worked out in practice. Suppose a man was seen on the sabbath engaged in some occupation which was traditionally regarded as prohibited 'work', and suppose that those who saw him were a group of two or three persons well qualified in the law. They would first inform him that his action was illegal: this would constitute a formal warning, and if the man did not observe it, he would be committing a 'presumptuous sin'.[7] If he persevered, they would then question him to discover whether there was any factor in the case which would make it an exception to the normal rule (such as that the 'work' needed to be done urgently in order to save a life). If there were no such factor, the case would be clear, and it would be the duty of the witnesses to see that the sanctions laid down in the law were carried out. It would be sufficient for them to call upon a few 'elders'—that is, reputable citizens—to make up the required 'court'. But the function of these 'judges' was minimal. It was the witnesses themselves who played the important role. They had the evidence of their own eyes—checked, if necessary, against each other's observations—that the defendant had (shall we say) been seen

[7] M. Sanh. 5.1; M. Makk. 1.8, 9.

carrying a bed on the sabbath;[8] they will have known precisely the law governing such actions, and established that in this case the defendant could plead no special circumstances. They will also have known what punishment was laid down in such cases; and since it was the duty of the witnesses to inflict the penalty, they would actually have been failing by their duty to the law if they did not personally see to it that the sentence was carried out.

Of course, this was a risky procedure. If, in their role as witnesses, they had failed to make exactly certain of the facts; if, in their role as judges, they had failed to remember a particular clause of the law bearing upon the case; or if, in their role as executioners, they failed to carry out the sentence correctly, they might be in grave personal danger. Therefore they might well prefer to take the case to a regular court of practised judges. But even there, they would be the principal and perhaps the only witnesses. There were grave penalties for giving false evidence.[9] And they would still have the duty of seeing that the sentence was carried out. Under these circumstances many people might well have preferred to drop the case altogether. But anyone really concerned with the proper observance of the law was bound to recognize his obligation to enforce it by any means within his power.

In the light of this, let us consider Jesus' encounter with 'the Jews' (who, in John's Gospel, stand for precisely the type of person we have been considering) on the occasion of Jesus' first visit to Jerusalem during a festival (John 5.1). Jesus had cured a cripple by the sheep-pool,[10] with the result that 'the man recovered instantly, took up his stretcher, and began to walk' (5.9). But it was the sabbath—a point mentioned only

---

[8] This type of act was regarded as a prohibited work already in Jer. 17.21; it is expressly forbidden in M. Shab. 10.5.

[9] In theory at least, a comparable penalty to that which would have been sustained by the defendant if convicted. cf. M. Sanh. 11.6. Josephus *Ant.* IV, 219.

[10] For a recent study of the location of this episode, and an interesting suggestion that it took place in a pagan sanctuary, see A. Duprez, *Jésus et les dieux guérisseurs* (1970).

now by the narrator, since only now does it become important.
'So the Jews said to the man who had been cured, "It is the
Sabbath. You are not allowed to carry your bed on the Sabbath".' This constituted a formal warning: if he continued
to carry it he would be 'sinning presumptuously'. But the man
had a special reason to offer: the command to carry his bed
had been part of the act by which he had been cured (5.8);
therefore (as the Jews recognized when they went on to ask
him, 'Who is the man who told you to take up your bed and
walk?' 5.12), the responsibility lay with him who had effected
the cure. And this led to the first really serious confrontation
between Jesus and the Jews which John recounts as
follows:

> It was works of this kind done on the Sabbath that stirred
> the Jews to persecute Jesus. He defended himself by say-
> ing, 'My Father has never yet ceased his work, and I am
> working too.' This made the Jews still more determined to
> kill him, because he was not only breaking the Sabbath, but,
> by calling God his own Father, he claimed equality with
> God (John 5.16–18).

This short paragraph repays careful analysis. The point of
departure is that Jesus had publicly, and on several occasions,
healed sick people on the sabbath (and the Synoptic Gospels
confirm that this was an absolutely characteristic activity of
Jesus). No group of responsible and earnest Jews could let this
pass: on the face of it, Jesus had repeatedly broken the third
commandment, and they would be failing in their duty if
they did not see to it that the offender was convicted and
punished. As already explained, it was not necessary for them
to bring the case before a formal court: they were competent
to initiate proceedings themselves. This is precisely the situation envisaged by the evangelist: 'It was works of this kind
done on the Sabbath that stirred the Jews to persecute Jesus.'
This is the usual translation; but in this context the English
word 'persecute' is inappropriate. The Jews in John's Gospel
are not irrational. They do not conceive a kind of blind hatred

against Jesus, and start 'persecuting' him for his beliefs or
his attitudes. In fact, in this context the word translated
'persecute' bears a different meaning. The word is perfectly
good Greek[11] for 'bring a charge against', 'prosecute'. This
is the meaning here. The Jews had observed Jesus apparently
breaking the law, and it was their religious duty to bring a
charge against him, to convict him and to punish him. As we
have seen, this was a responsible and sometimes risky enter-
prise. But it was entirely to be expected that they should
undertake it; and John expresses this correctly and idiomati-
cally[12] in the words, 'They sought to bring a charge against
him'.

Jesus' answer, 'My father has never yet ceased his work, and
I am working too', is of the same type as his replies to similar
charges in the Synoptic Gospels:[13] sabbath regulations in
themselves are not sufficient to determine God's will for men
under all possible circumstances. Jesus endorses what was later
to become a standard rabbinic view[14] that God continues to
'work' in some sense despite his own 'Sabbath rest' which
followed the completion of his creation (Gen. 2.2); and he
implicitly claims this supreme authority for his own action.[15]
In other words, Jesus had indeed a defence, in the form of
a reason why it was right for him to perform an act which
was *prima facie* a transgression of the law relating to the
sabbath; but this defence depended on there being a special
relationship between himself and God—that is, on him being
the Son of God in a very much more personal and individual
sense than that according to which any Jew might call upon

[11] διώκειν. LSJ cites instances from Herodotus to Appian, but,
like all other lexica, translations, and commentaries I have seen, cites
John 5.16 under the sense 'to persecute'.

[12] ἐδίωκον is a 'conative imperfect', on which see Moulton,
Grammar of N.T. Greek I, 128–9; Goodwin, *Moods and Tenses*, §36.

[13] He gives a further reply to the same (implied) charge in 7.23–4,
which is still more reminiscent of the Synoptics.

[14] Exod. R. 30.6; Gen. R. 11.12.

[15] On the background to this argument see Dodd, *Interpretation*,
321–8, and p. 90 below.

God as 'Father'. This defence was a dangerous one. For how could Jesus prove that it was true? And if it were not true, then his words amounted to a more serious offence even than that of transgressing the sabbath: he would be committing blasphemy.[16] And the penalty for blasphemy was death.

The evangelist's comment on this is as follows: 'This made the Jews still more determined to kill him.' Two capital offences presented an easier challenge to Jews concerned for the observance of the law, and made their action still more necessary—this is how many readers of the Gospel will have understood this sentence, since according to the Bible (Num. 15.35) both sabbath-breaking[17] and blasphemy carried the death penalty. But it may be that a closer knowledge of contemporary Pharisaism is required here; for the Pharisees, besides codifying the activities which could be regarded as permissible on the sabbath, also appear to have recognized a milder penalty than death by stoning in certain cases.[18] If this is in mind, the evangelist's words may have greater precision: 'the Jews therefore pressed their attack against him with a view rather to killing him[19] [on a charge of blasphemy, than to exacting the sin-offering which might have been the only consequence of his sabbath-breaking]'. At any rate, John is correctly reporting the serious turn which events had taken now that Jesus had made the apparently blasphemous claim that God was his own, personal Father.

On this occasion nothing further happened. But now, as we might put it, the machinery of justice had started to turn, and there could be no looking back. A group of Jews had heard Jesus uttering blasphemy, and it was their clear duty to judge him, to condemn him, and to execute him (all, as we have seen, proper functions for the same group of people). They had,

[16] On the definition of this offence, see pp. 77–81 below.
[17] This was recognized in different sections of Judaism; cf. Jub. 2.27; M. Sanh. 7.4.
[18] M. Sanh. 7.8; cf. M. Ker. 4.1–2. A milder penalty is also permitted in the Damascus Document, CD 12.3–4.
[19] μᾶλλον ἐζήτουν ... ἀποκτεῖναι.

of course, to make sure that certain conditions were fulfilled. There must be no inconsistencies in their evidence that Jesus had spoken the incriminating words; it must be clear that his utterance fell within the definition of blasphemy; and it must be physically possible for them to carry out the sentence. On the first point there was no doubt: Jesus had spoken publicly, and all were agreed about what he had said. But the other two conditions were less easily fulfilled—there was uncertainty about the exact blasphemous content of Jesus' words, and about the practicality of having him put to death. It is these two conditions which provide the dramatic framework for a number of the episodes which follow.

The story continues with Jesus' next appearance in Jerusalem. The Jews, of course, already have their evidence; but they need a more clearly-defined instance of blasphemy to work on, and they need an opportunity to carry out the sentence. Jesus now seems to provide them with the first, by crying aloud as he teaches in the temple, 'I was sent by the One who truly is, and him you do not know. I know him because I come from him and he it is who sent me' (7.28). Once again, this is a terrific claim. Either it is true, or it is blasphemous. The Jewish experts naturally assume that it is not true, and so must take the action necessary to punish a blasphemer. The text goes on: 'At this they tried to seize him'—and had it been possible they would doubtless have inflicted the death penalty. But now John introduces the first of a series of factors which were to prevent this again and again. This time it is a mysterious—we might say a theological —one: 'No one laid a hand on him because his appointed hour had not yet come.'

The pattern is now beginning to establish itself: utterance of blasphemous words, attempt to seize or punish, unexpected obstacle to the course of justice. The next instance conforms precisely: Jesus said, 'If you knew me, you would know my Father as well' (8.19)—another clear case of a claim that was either true or blasphemous. The text goes on: 'These words were spoken by Jesus in the treasury as he taught in the temple. Yet no one arrested him, because his hour had not yet come'—the same mysterious impediment as before, preventing the natural completion of the trial, and allowing the story to continue.

And continue it does, right through the chapter, until Jesus finally makes a statement so clear that his judges can no longer feel any doubt: 'In very truth I tell you, before Abraham was born, I am.' This time the reaction is immediate. 'They picked up stones to throw at him.' The penalty for blasphemy was death by stoning, and since Jesus' blasphemy seemed undeniable and had been clearly heard, it was the responsibility of the qualified witnesses to cast the first stone. The only thing which saved Jesus' life this time was a mysterious elusiveness. 'But Jesus was not to be seen; and he left the temple' (8.59).

We still have not finished. In chapter 10, Jesus is again in the temple, and again makes the kind of statement which can leave no doubt in the minds of his judges: 'My Father and I are one' (10.30). The narrative goes on—as we know it must—'Once again the Jews picked up stones to stone him.' This time Jesus interrupts the process by calling into question their definition of blasphemy. His point appears to be a valid one; but he goes on to put his original statement in a form still more startlingly blasphemous (if it was not true): 'The Father is in me, and I in the Father.' John goes on: 'This provoked them to one more attempt to seize him. But he escaped from their clutches.' The mysterious impediment was still there, preventing the completion of the trial, and allowing the story to continue. Of course, as we know, the impediment was not there much longer. The Jews were soon to succeed in seizing him. But even when they had done so, there was still a difficulty. As they said to Pilate, they were not allowed to put any man to death (18.31).

Pilate said, 'Take him away and try him by your own law.'

The Jews answered, 'We are not allowed to put any man to death'.

From the point of view of history this remark (which occurs only in John's Gospel) is exceedingly important: it is the key to understanding why Jesus was crucified by the Romans instead of stoned by the Jews. Without it, we would be able to make little sense of the passion story in any of the Gospels. But in the context of John's Gospel, its significance is rather different. It is the last of those mysterious impediments which had prevented justice from taking its normal course. In reality it may have been in the nature of an excuse. The Jews had certainly intended to put Jesus to death on previous occasions. But the sympathies of the crowd, and the very elusiveness of Jesus, had frustrated them again and again. If the rules of the Roman administration did not officially permit them to carry out the penalty anyway, they may have finally accepted with relief this way out of the difficulty. Their zeal for the Jewish law would be satisfied so long as Pilate could be persuaded to inflict the death penalty.

Even from this brief analysis, one fact is already clear: the natural western assumption that a formal court is necessary for legal proceedings to take place does not hold for the world in which Jesus lived; and there are a number of occasions in John's Gospel (compared with the single occasion in the Synoptics) on which Jesus was actually on trial as the defendant on a charge of either sabbath-breaking or blasphemy, and it was only a combination of special circumstances which prevented judgement being completed and the sentence being carried out. But what was true of criminal cases was true to a still greater extent of civil cases. If a man wished to settle a dispute or to establish a claim, it was sufficient for him to find a person or persons whom his adversary would accept and who was competent to judge the admissibility of his evidence. No formal court or official procedures were necessary: the boundary between informal controversy and litigation was often hard to draw.

It follows that in tracing the 'trial' of Jesus through the Fourth Gospel we must look not only at the occasions on which Jesus was the defendant on a charge; we must consider

also those in which he was a claimant whose claim was being
challenged and who needed to have it formally established.
One of the clearest instances of this is in John 8.12–20. 'Jesus
said, I am the light of the world. No follower of mine shall
wander in the dark ...'. This is, of course, a tremendous
claim. Exactly what the claim amounts to is not perhaps the
most important question for the moment. The language is
highly pictorial. At different moments in the Gospel Jesus
describes himself as the true bread, as living water, as light,
as life. Each of these great poetical images gives the reader a
new insight into the ultimate significance of Jesus; and their
effect is cumulative: one should not concentrate on one of
them to the exclusion of the others. But the fact which binds
them together is that they are all ways of making a single
stupendous claim. The Light of the World—like all the other
great images—is language appropriate to no ordinary man.
By using it, Jesus is claiming to be someone unique and
authoritative.

On this occasion, the initial response of those before whom
the claim is made is a technical one. 'You are giving evidence
about yourself.' Therefore, 'your evidence is not valid'.[20] In
other words, you are making a great claim, but you can produce no witness, no evidence, to substantiate it. Without such
a witness, or such evidence, we cannot believe and accept your
claim. How was Jesus to answer this point? A moment's
thought will show us the problem. How could he produce a
witness to his extraordinary claim? There was no one who
could say, 'I happen to know that Jesus is the light of the
world'; and what document or exhibit could possibly exist
which would prove Jesus to be what he said he was? As Jesus
said himself, 'I know where I come from and where I am going,
but you do not know either where I come from or where I

---

[20] $\dot{\alpha}\lambda\eta\theta\acute{\eta}\varsigma$ cf. p. 20 above. Jewish courts were neither concerned
nor equipped to establish whether evidence was (in our sense) 'true',
but only whether it was admissible and trustworthy. 'Valid' or perhaps
'reliable' would convey the sense.

am going' (8.14). In other words, the case was one of those
mentioned earlier, where only the claimant has knowledge
of the relevant facts and where no independent evidence is
available. The judges simply have to make up their minds
whether or not to accept the word of the claimant before them.
What Jesus actually replied was, 'Even if I do give evidence
about myself, my evidence is valid'. From the point of view
of procedure, this was quite correct.

But now, yet one more feature of the Jewish system must
be noticed. Strange though it may seem to us, one consequence
of the informality of proceedings which we have been studying
was that it was not always clear who was judging whom: the
tables might actually be turned as the case progressed. Or to
put it another way: cases were tried not only before men, but
also before God (Exod. 22.8–9), and if either party were prepared to bring God in (so to speak) on his side—that is, if
he were prepared to swear on oath that his testimony was
true—then grave consequences followed. His oath might be
false, in which case God would punish him (this was devoutly
believed); but in the absence of any sign of divine wrath, the
human 'judges' must assume the evidence to be true, and if
they failed to accept it, they would themselves stand to be
judged by the erst-while claimant. The claimant would not, of
course, come with this intention in the first place; but if those
to whom he was appealing to accept his claim refused to
believe him, even when he 'called God to witness', he was
bound to 'judge' them himself.

This is exactly what is happening in the episode we are
studying. Jesus' claim is made (under the circumstances) perfectly correctly; but his judges will not accept it. Jesus does
not come with the intention of judging anyone[21] (8.15); but
when he is disbelieved, he has no option but to judge; and he
goes on (again quite correctly) to define the conditions under
which this judging must take place. He would not become the

---

[21] $\dot{\epsilon}\gamma\dot{\omega}$ $o\dot{\upsilon}$ $\kappa\rho\dot{\iota}\nu\omega$ $o\dot{\upsilon}\delta\dot{\epsilon}\nu\alpha$: an 'habitual' or 'iterative' present:
Moulton, *Grammar of N.T. Greek* I, 119.

judge at all unless he knew that God (who is of course present at all proceedings) was on his side; and so he says, 'But if I do judge, it is the fact that I am not alone, but have with me him who sent me, which makes my judgement valid' (8.16). For now the rules are different. So long as he was simply a claimant, his case rested on his own word alone—we have seen how this was allowable under these very special circumstances. But now that he is judge and prosecutor, he must have supporting evidence: in Jewish law no charge could be preferred without at least two witnesses (Deut. 17.6). Jesus acknowledges the point himself: 'In your own law it is written that there have to be two witnesses for evidence to be valid.' What witness can Jesus invoke? 'My father who sent me', Jesus replies; and the Jews, in a way characteristic of the Gospel, are made to jump to the wrong conclusion: they assume he means his human father, whose evidence of course would be valueless, since you were not allowed to get your own close relatives into court to testify for you. In fact, of course, Jesus is calling on a much more powerful witness. His real father is God. And calling God to witness is equivalent to swearing a solemn oath. If his opponents disbelieve that, they will have condemned themselves. It was as dangerous to disbelieve a statement made on oath as to make a statement on oath that was not true. As is said earlier in the Gospel, 'God did not send his son into the world that he should judge the world. He who believes in him is not judged; but he who does not believe is judged already.' Jesus is on trial, yes; but this cannot happen without the risk of his judges being on trial too.

All this is distinctively Johannine. No other New Testament writer presents Jesus as caught in a long-drawn-out legal action provoked in the first place by certain of his words and deeds. But equally, no other writer offers so compelling an account of the reasons why Jesus was brought to trial by his fellow-Jews: the sequence of events, in John's Gospel, seems rooted in the normal and necessary observance by Jews of their own legal system in a way unparalleled in the other Gospels. It is time, as in previous chapters, to turn to them and consider their evidence.

One difference is so obvious that it is noticed at once. Whereas in John's Gospel (as we have seen) there is a long sequence of episodes in which legal terminology is used and in which legal proceedings appear to be initiated, in the Synoptics there is only one 'trial', that which begins before Caiaphas and ends before Pilate. We must consider the implication of this in a moment. But first, there is a still more fundamental difference to notice. In John, as we have seen, the opposition to Jesus takes the form of a correct response to his works and deeds on the part of those who are concerned to maintain the proper observance of the law: Jesus does or says something which is *prima facie* a breach of the law, and those who have witnessed the alleged offence seek to establish their charge, to procure a judgement from their fellow-elders, and to carry out the sentence. Again and again they are frustrated, but this does not affect the fact that certain things said or done by Jesus have laid upon them (as they think) an obligation to proceed against him. Very different is the account in Mark. There, after Jesus' arrest (which is the kind of action normally taken, not against a citizen who has broken the law, but against a totally lawless insurrectionary,[22]) there is no setting up of a formal trial, since there appears to be no charge on which to proceed. The hearing in fact begins, not as a trial at all, but as an attempt to frame a charge which would justify the arrest which has taken place and any proceedings which might follow. 'They began to look for evidence against Jesus on which to put him to death' (Mark 14.55)—the phrase is almost identical with that in John 5.18, but describes a totally different situation in that here (unlike the situation in John) no clear charge has been established and there is no agreement about what the charge should be. To put the matter somewhat crudely, the proceedings at this stage are not those of a 'trial' at all, but of a police investigation designed to reveal

---

[22] ὡς ἐπὶ λῃστήν Mark 14.48.

the charge under which a suspect may be brought before a court.[23]

Yet (since the judicial and political authorities were one and the same in Jewish society) there were plenty of qualified 'judges' there; and the hearing could turn into a 'trial' the moment Jesus was heard by all to make a self-incriminating statement. This, indeed, is precisely what the authorities (having failed to substantiate a charge themselves) endeavoured to elicit. Their first attempts were unsuccessful: 'Jesus was silent and made no answer' (14.61)—as he had a perfect right to do, since no charge had been made against him. But then, surprisingly, they were successful. 'The high priest asked him, Are you the Christ?'. According to Matthew, the question was still more pointed, in that Jesus was asked to answer it on oath.[24] This may be correct. But either way, the surprising thing is that Jesus yielded to the request. He affirmed (or at least, if we follow Matthew,[25] he did not deny) that he was indeed the Christ, and added a prediction that the Son of Man oracle in Daniel 7.13 would shortly be fulfilled. This, it seems, was immediately recognized as blasphemy. The high priest performed the correct action of rending his clothes, and appealed to the judgement of the others. No doubts were expressed, either about the fact of Jesus' blasphemy or its legal consequences. By virtue of their standing and their expert knowledge, those present formed a qualified court. They passed judgement and sentence; and we assume that had they been able to they would have carried out the sentence themselves.

---

[23] When Mark states in 14.53 that 'all the high priests and elders and scribes came together' and in 14.55 that 'the high priests and the whole council (συνέδριον) tried to find evidence ...' it is usually assumed that he is describing a formal session of the Sanhedrin sitting as a court, even though it was unheard of for such a session to take place in the high priest's house and at night. This may be so. But, as we have seen, the distinction is in reality less sharp than is usually thought; and in any case, Mark nowhere states this to have been a formal sitting of a court.

[24] ἐξορκίζω σε, Matt. 26.63.

[25] σὺ εἶπας, Matt. 26.64.

This account, though very different from anything in John's Gospel, is plausible enough in its own right. Jesus was a suspect and possibly dangerous person. It was prudent of the Jewish authorities to arrest him (for they had an interest in preserving order on behalf of the Romans); and the attempt to frame a charge against him was the natural thing to do under the circumstances. But (and this can easily escape notice) having secured their evidence from Jesus' own lips, it was not necessary to convene a separate sitting of the 'court'. Those who had been summoned to the high priest's house were the kind of people who were fully competent in the law—indeed, they represented, and may even have included, most of the members of the three classes which made up the Sanhedrin when it sat as the supreme Jewish council in Jerusalem. There was nothing (other than the constraint apparently laid upon them by the Roman administration) to prevent them proceeding immediately to judgement, conviction, sentence, and execution. It is true, of course, that all this would have been impossible had the rules subsequently formulated in the Mishnah been strictly applied. According to these, a hearing at night was illegal, a second hearing would have been necessary before the sentence was carried out, and in any case the approach of the Passover would have made an adjournment essential.[26] These rules are often invoked to cast doubt upon the historicity of Mark's narrative. But it is far from certain that they were in force before the fall of Jerusalem, or, even if they were, that they would have been observed in an emergency; and on the other side one must set, not only the episode of an immediate judicial execution of Stephen by a Jewish assembly,[27] but also those occasions in John's Gospel, already studied, where an agreement that Jesus had uttered blasphemy was followed immediately by an attempt to stone him to death. Once the preliminary investigation has been detached from it, the 'trial' of Jesus

[26] M. Sanh. 4.1.

[27] Acts 7.57. The fact that this was illegal *officially* does not mean that they may not have tried to get away with it on occasion. cf. pp. 4, 55 above.

in Mark (consisting of blasphemy by Jesus, agreement on the facts of the case among those present, judgement, sentence, and attempted execution) is entirely of a type with the episodes which we have been studying in John.

Of a type, perhaps; but the actual occasion is, of course, entirely different. In John, the issue has been brought to a head several times already, and after Jesus' arrest there is no need to go through it all again: the interview with Annas (John 18.19–24) is an entirely informal investigation. But in Mark, it is clear that there has been no such preparation. Only after the arrest does the issue of blasphemy arise, and Jesus' decisive words are elicited in the course of a hearing which is (or at least which easily becomes) a formal trial under the presidency of the high priest. In John's Gospel, despite the succession of trial scenes which lead up to the arrest, there is no episode strictly corresponding to the trial scene in Mark and Matthew.

But a word must be said about the evidence of Luke. Luke's account departs from those of Mark and Matthew, in that it places the critical trial scene, not during the night when Jesus was held in the high priest's house, but after dawn in some other place where competent judges were assembled.[28] This arrangement, though it is perhaps less plausible in the light of subsequent events,[29] conforms better with the procedure subsequently laid down in the Mishnah, in that the trial takes place by daylight and is presumably held in the normal court-room. But in other respects the procedure runs if anything even less by the book. Nothing is said about the high priest presiding; and Jesus' reply to the question, 'Are you the Son of God?' seems even more ambiguous than in the other Gospels ('It is you who say that I am'). Indeed, the whole scene has something of the informality (as we feel it to be) of the scenes we have been studying in John.

It is therefore all the more significant that striking verbal

---

[28] 22.66, ἀπήγαγον αὐτὸν εἰς τὸ συνέδριον αὐτῶν.

[29] cf. A. N. Sherwin-White, *Roman Society and Roman Law in the N.T.*, 45: 'The Jews would have been too late to catch Pilate at his early morning *Levée.*'

similarities exist between this trial scene in Luke and an earlier but critical episode in John. It will be useful to quote the two passages side by side.

i Luke 22.66–71.

When day broke, the elders of the nation, chief priests, and doctors of the law assembled, and he was brought before their Council. 'Tell us,' they said, 'are you the Messiah?' 'If I tell you,' he replied, 'you will not believe me; and if I ask questions, you will not answer. But from now on, the Son of Man will be seated at the right hand of Almighty God' 'You are the Son of God, then?' they all said, and he replied, 'It is you who say I am'. They said, 'Need we call further witnesses? We have heard it ourselves from his own lips.'

ii John 10.24–33

The Jews gathered round him and asked: 'How long must you keep us in suspense? If you are the Messiah say so plainly.' 'I have told you,' said Jesus, 'but you do not believe.... My Father and I are one.' Once again the Jews picked up stones to stone him.... The Jews replied, 'We are not going to stone you for any good deed, but for your blasphemy. You, a mere man, claim to be God.'

The similarities are striking. In Luke, Jesus is asked, 'Are you the Christ? Tell us.' In John, 'If you are the Christ, tell us plainly.' In Luke, Jesus replies, 'If I tell you, you will not believe me.' In John, 'I have told you, but you do not believe.' In Luke, they ask, 'You are the Son of God then?'; Jesus answers, 'It is you who say I am', and they regard his offence as established. In John, Jesus says, 'My Father and I are one,' and the Jews, regarding his blasphemy as established, seek to inflict the penalty. Clearly, the drift of the dialogue is the same in each case, and many of the phrases are almost identical. At the very least, we may infer that it is a recollection of the same or a similar incident which lies behind both accounts.[30] Only the setting is different: in Luke, a formal

[30] This is the conclusion of Dodd, *HTFG*, 91f.

meeting of the authorities; in John, a chance encounter in the temple.

Yet we have seen that it may be misleading to press even this distinction too hard. In none of the Gospel accounts is the 'trial' of Jesus explicitly described as a judicial session of the Sanhedrin; indeed, in Mark and Matthew it begins, not as a trial at all, but as an investigation intended to establish a charge on which the prisoner may be brought to trial. Only when Jesus utters words which are held to be blasphemous do the assembled experts constitute themselves a 'court' competent to pronounce verdict and sentence; and in Luke, where the time and place are at least more compatible with a normal trial, the membership of the court is less precisely defined[31] ('high priests and scribes', 'their council' (*synhedrion*), 'the whole crowd of them'). In other words, the Synoptic Gospels by no means force us to conclude that Jesus was tried at a formal session of the Sanhedrin, specially convened to try a capital case.

Moreover, there are details in John's account which narrow the gap still further. 'Jesus was walking in the temple precincts, in Solomon's Portico.' This is a vivid and significant *mise en scène*. The temple building stood on an immense terrace which had been restored and enlarged by Herod the Great. On three sides of this open space stood great porticos or *stoas*—the technical name for long narrow buildings, open on one side, the roof supported by one or more rows of pillars—one of which was known as 'Solomon's'. These *stoas* were as regular a feature of the eastern cities of the Roman Empire as the town halls or the railway stations of our cities today; and everyone knew what they were for. They served for informal meetings, for business and commerce; they served for teaching, preaching, and political discussions; and they served on occasion as law courts. It was natural for Jesus to be in such

---

[31] Too much should not be made of the fact that in Matthew and Mark the high priest presides. This may have been the natural thing under the circumstances, but even the Mishnah does not specify who should preside when capital cases are tried.

a place as a teacher; it was equally natural for a group of responsible Jews to approach him there.

But it was an approach of a particular kind. The Greek word is usually translated by a phrase such as 'They gathered round him' (NEB). But the word is more aggressive. Literally, 'they surrounded him', like an army encircling a besieged city, or (more significantly) a court gathered in a semi-circle round an accused man.[32] And indeed, as we have seen, the episode which follows is nothing less than a trial. The charge and the evidence are the same as those in Luke's narrative. The verdict in each case is death, and only Jesus' mysterious elusiveness saves him from immediate execution. There turns out to be less difference in substance between this 'trial' of Jesus in John and the 'trial' of Jesus in Luke than might appear at first sight.

There is, however, a further important difference between John and the Synoptics. In John, as we have seen, the issue on which Jesus incurs the judgement of his law-abiding contemporaries, and is again and again brought to trial by them, is, first, his alleged breach of the sabbath regulations, and then (and thereafter always) his statements to the effect that he has a special and unique relationship with the Father, that he is 'the Son of God'. In the Synoptics, the question of the sabbath does indeed arise, and is a prominent theme, though (as we shall see in the next chapter) it does not arise in such a way as to precipitate legal proceedings. But in the matter of Jesus' claim to be the Son of God, there is a very definite difference of treatment. In John, Jesus' claim is the spring of the action in a number of episodes; but in the Synoptics, the opposition to Jesus is attributed to other less technical motives (fear, jealousy, political expediency), and the Son of God issue arises only at the end, in the course of the 'trial' before Caiaphas. But, once again, the points of contact turn out to be more frequent than appears at first sight. The Synoptic Gospels are by no means ignorant of Jesus' claims to be the Son of God.

[32] ἐκύκλωσαν; cf. M. Sanh. 4.3: 'The Sanhedrin sat in the form of a semi-circle.'

On the contrary, both Matthew and Luke preserve the saying (which is commonly noticed to have a Johannine flavour), 'Everything is entrusted to me by my Father ...' (Matt. 11.26–7; Luke 10.21–2): this contains an explicit claim on the part of Jesus to be the unique Son of God. Again, the words, 'About that day or that hour no one knows, ... not even the Son; only the Father' (Mark 13.32; Matt. 24.36) appear to make the same claim. The issue, it is true, is expressed most clearly in the statement in John's Gospel of the Jews to Pilate, 'We have a law; and by that law he ought to die, because he has claimed to be Son of God' (John 19.7). But exactly the same point underlies the Jews' mockery in Matthew 27.43, 'Let God rescue him, if he wants him—for he said he was God's Son.' The same tradition, that Jesus claimed to be the Son of God, is preserved in all the Gospels, even if it is only in the Fourth that it becomes a mainspring of the action.

With this we reach what is perhaps the most important point established so far. We have noticed the different ways in which John and the Synoptics approach the 'trial' of Jesus; but we have noticed also significant points of agreement. In particular, it has appeared that in all the accounts there are two issues of a legal nature which precipitate a confrontation between Jesus and the Jews: healing on the sabbath, and using words and titles (such as 'Son of God') which were held to be blasphemous. At the very least, we have gained further historical information about Jesus of considerable reliability. That Jesus performed acts which were held to be a breach of the fourth commandment, and that he uttered words which, because of their apparently blasphemous character, were punishable (according to the Jewish law) by death, seem to be facts that are implicit in all our accounts, and without which the condemnation of Jesus by the Jews would be incomprehensible. Having considered in some detail the procedure under which these charges could be brought and heard, it is time to give closer attention to the charges themselves.

4

The Charges

THE SABBATH

The Gospels record two types of action for which Jesus was responsible which were *prima facie* violations of the sabbath: plucking ears of corn, and healing. In every case but one these actions brought Jesus into conflict with the Jewish authorities, and attention is focused, both in the Gospel accounts themselves and in modern discussion of these episodes, on the arguments with which Jesus appears to have confounded his opponents. Since it was almost invariably the words and actions of Jesus himself, rather than the circumstances which elicited them, that were treasured and pondered by the early Church, this emphasis is understandable. But for a full understanding of the events which underlie the Gospel narratives it is essential to start with some account of the legal background.

The point of departure for the laws concerning the sabbath was the clause in Exodus 31.15, 'Anyone who does work [on the sabbath day] shall be cut off from his father's kin.' The types of work envisaged by this law may originally have been agricultural,[1] but at various times different movements within Judaism tended to include more and more human activities under the general heading of prohibited 'work': the Maccabean warriors had been prepared to sacrifice even their own safety to their concern not to violate the sabbath by waging war on it;[2] and it seems that the Essenes interpreted the prohibition so strictly that virtually all household tasks were forbidden.[3] The Pharisees' approach was less extreme than this,

---

[1] cf. Jewish Encyclopaedia s.v. 'Sabbath'; Derrett, *Jesus's Audience*, 73-4.
[2] I Macc. 2.32-8.
[3] Josephus, *B.J.* II, 147.

though we know from the Mishnah that there existed a list of thirty-nine separate types of prohibited work.[4] The effect of this, however, was not necessarily to increase the severity of the law; for the tendency of Pharisaic legislation was so far as possible to protect the individual from the risk of transgressing a commandment of the law of Moses and incurring thereby the statutory punishment of death. That is to say: if the penalty for a certain type of offence was death, it was essential to know exactly when one was in danger of committing it; the greater the precision which the courts could bring to bear on the matter, the greater the safety of the individual. Moreover, the Pharisees appear to have succeeded in limiting the death-penalty to cases where the offence was both deliberate and flagrant, and in substituting a lesser penalty for cases of inadvertent transgression.[5]

It is not of course certain that it was this Pharisaic legislation which was already the basis of court decisions in cases of sabbath violation in the time of Jesus; but even if this was not so, the penalties for this offence, and the risk of committing it, would hardly have been less serious; indeed it was the tendency of the Pharisees (as we have seen) to mitigate the severity of the law in this matter.[6] We are therefore in a position to ask, what were the legal consequences of committing the two kinds of sabbath offence of which Jesus or his disciples were accused—plucking corn and healing the sick? It will be seen at once that this is a practical question: if a certain act was committed, what procedures were necessary for the offender to be convicted, what mitigating circumstances might be advanced, and what would be the normal sentence? It is a

---

[4] All allegedly derived from the premiss that work on the Tabernacle was interrupted on the sabbath, an inference from the juxtaposition of Exod. 35.4 with Exod. 35.1–3.

[5] M. Sanh. 7.8: many deliberate acts were subject, not to the death penalty, but to *Kareth*, i.e. the risk of direct punishment by God; while acts committed inadvertently involved only a sin-offering. See p. 52 above.

[6] cf. H. E. Goldin, *Hebrew Criminal Law and Procedure* (1952), 24–5.

very different question from the much more academic one
which appears to dominate the discussion, both in the Gospel
narratives and in modern commentaries, namely, whether the
laws then in force on this subject were good and equitable. The
difference can easily be illustrated by a modern analogy. Large
protest marches in cities have recently become a frequent
occurrence. They tend to come into conflict with a number
of laws concerned with maintaining civil order and protecting
private property, laws which were not for the most part
designed to cope with demonstrations on this scale. Public
discussion of the consequences of such marches (for the police,
for the participants, for the rights of the various parties) will
tend to be 'academic', in that it will concentrate on the alleged
justice or injustice of the existing laws and their application
by the courts through the police. Yet underlying this discussion it will be essential that everyone concerned should know
what the state of the law is at present and what legal consequences will follow from certain actions. Very much the
same goes for Jesus' actions on the sabbath. Discussion naturally centres on the apparent irksomeness and inhumanity of
the legislation then in force. But it is essential to know also
the extent to which Jesus and his followers were exposing
themselves to the possibility of action in a court of law.

We may begin with the plucking of corn on the sabbath
by Jesus' disciples. One of the few explicit references in the
Bible to the 'work' prohibited on the sabbath clearly refers
to ploughing and reaping (Exod. 34.21); and that this was
generally interpreted to mean even the plucking of a few ears
is confirmed, not just by subsequent talmudic tradition,[7] but
by a chance reference in Philo.[8] We need have no doubt,
therefore, that the action of Jesus' disciples was clearly illegal;
but Mark does not explain why they did it. Ignorance seems
an unlikely pretext: the activity was one of the most basic
of those prohibited on the sabbath. Nor does it seem likely

---

[7] S-B I, 617.
[8] *De Vita Mosis* II, 22 οὐ γὰρ ἔρνος, οὐ κλάδον, ἀλλ' οὐδὲ πέταλον
ἐφεῖται τεμεῖν κτλ.

that they chose this way of being deliberately provocative: provocation of this kind is characteristic, not of the disciples, but of Jesus, and then only for a humanitarian reason. We are left with only one possibility, and this is stated to have been the case in Matthew (12.1): the disciples were genuinely hungry. We may suppose that, having had no money, or no opportunity, to lay in supplies on the Friday afternoon, and being in a strange town and receiving no hospitality, they went a few hundred yards[9] into the nearest cornfield to chew some grains of corn,[10] and so make their hunger more bearable until sundown, when, the sabbath being over, it would again be permissible to buy or beg some food. Jesus accompanied them, though it is implied that he did not share their hunger to the extent of committing the crime himself. But, being their acknowledged master, it was he, rather than the disciples,[11] who was challenged for their action.

The words of the challenge are recorded with little variation in the three Synoptic Gospels: 'Why are they doing what is illegal on the Sabbath?' It is possible that Mark has preserved an Aramaic idiom (the exclamatory *mah*) which suggests, not just a question, but an expression of indignation: 'Whatever do they think they are doing, transgressing the Sabbath?'[12] But in any case, it was the correct reaction for witnesses of their standing (all the accounts state that they were Pharisees). In effect, they were giving a formal warning, after which any further offence would be punishable; and, as we

[9] Not more than a 'sabbath day's journey', either for themselves or for their witnesses.

[10] This would have been perfectly legal on any other day—Deut. 23.25. The custom was observed among Arabs in Palestine at least until the nineteenth century; cf. E. Robinson, *Biblical Researches in Palestine* (1867) I, 493.

[11] Except in Luke (6.2), where nevertheless it is Jesus who answers the charge. The master was in fact responsible; cf. D. Daube, *NTS* 19 (1972), 1–15; J. Roloff, *Das Kerygma und der Irdische Jesus* (1970), 55f.

[12] M. Black, *An Aramaic Approach to the Gospels and Acts* (3e.), 122.

have seen, it was not necessary to convene a formal 'court' for this purpose, since we may assume that these Pharisees were fully competent to pass judgement themselves. They failed, however, to inquire whether there might be any special circumstances in this case which 'pushed aside' the sabbath; and it is upon this failure that Jesus fastens in his defence. There were special circumstances: just as David was able to put aside a legal prohibition because of being the special person he was (and just as—an additional argument advanced in Matthew—priests can officiate on the sabbath without violating it because of the special nature of their work), so Jesus could authorize his disciples to commit this exceptional transgression of the sabbath.[13] It is not recorded what his accusers thought of this argument: our accounts go straight on to record Jesus' general statement about the Son of Man being Lord of the Sabbath. In point of fact, it does not necessarily follow that there must have been any legal consequences: the 'court' may not have felt itself strong enough to pursue the matter, and may have contented itself with delivering a warning against any repetition of the action.[14] But the Gospels show no interest in that aspect of the matter. Only Matthew betrays a more technical approach: Jesus is made to say, 'Had you ... [taken certain considerations into account], you would not have convicted the innocent'. (12.7). The nuance is accurate. Whatever action it proposed to take, the court had reached a verdict of guilty before pausing to hear the evidence of the accused.

So far, then, the Gospel narratives show little interest in

[13] The reader is referred to the standard commentaries for a detailed discussion of Jesus' reply. E. Haenchen, *Der Weg Jesu*, 122–3, rightly protests against the dogmatic assertion of form critics since Bultmann that the story was invented or strongly moulded by the early Church when engaged in controversy with the synagogue over the observance of the sabbath. What is the evidence for such controversy? And why should such a bizarre instance have been chosen? So also J. Roloff, op. cit., 86–7.

[14] We do not know by what date the Pharisaic demand, that a formal warning should be given before a crime could lead to conviction, became effective; but it was probably before A.D. 70.

the legal consequences of Jesus' action on the sabbath. The case is different in the next episode, recorded immediately after in all three Synoptic Gospels. Jesus encountered a man with a withered hand in the synagogue; and some of those present (scribes and Pharisees, as Luke explains) were watching to see whether Jesus would cure him, 'so that they might frame an accusation against him' (Mark 3.2). Clearly this was not a matter of a warning: such an act of healing must have happened before, and a repetition would warrant a charge being brought. The Gospel narratives correctly describe the tension with which those legal experts watched Jesus to see whether, in their very presence, he would commit an offence which would furnish them with an immediate accusation to bring against him.

What would have been the nature of the charge? The prohibitions of 'work' elaborated in such detail in the Mishnah all envisage something being visibly or tangibly 'done'— objects being carried from place to place, men travelling or performing routine acts of physical work. If it was expected that Jesus would apply any physical remedies (as he occasionally did, using paste or spittle, or instructing the patient to go to a certain spring), then there would be a clear case, and it would be for Jesus to show that there was good reason (such as danger to life) for setting aside the sabbath. But in fact Jesus simply told the man to hold out his hand, which was immediately cured. It is difficult to see what regulation could have been infringed by this;[15] and indeed it may be that in reality Jesus' answer to his would-be accusers was to carry out the cure without making use of any of the usual medicinal or magical remedies. If so, then the short saying recorded by Mark and Luke gains considerable force. 'Is it permissible on the Sabbath to do good or to do evil, to save a life or to destroy it?' (Mark 3.4; Luke 6.9). Jesus' point is the characteristic one that the sabbath regulations alone do not prevent a man from doing evil, since evil is a matter of thoughts and

---

[15] The instances adduced by S-B I, (623–9) all involve physical action, e.g. M. Yoma 8.6—giving medicine.

words as much as of deeds (Mark 7.21–3). If it is 'legal' to do this kind of evil on the sabbath so long as no actual 'work' is done, it is obvious that it is 'legal' to do good. Jesus' anger (Mark 3.5) is then characteristic and easily explicable: his opponents were fussing about sabbath regulations when they should have been more concerned about the deeper springs of moral action.

On this interpretation, Jesus committed no indictable offence, and the reaction of his would-be judges was simply to 'take counsel against him' (Mark 3.6): Jesus had not acted in such a way as to warrant an indictment, and his challenge to the authorities did not concern a legal point. There is, however, an additional saying inserted at this point by Matthew:

> 'Suppose you had one sheep, which fell into a ditch on the Sabbath; is there one of you who would not catch hold of it and lift it out? And surely a man is worth far more than a sheep! It is therefore permitted to do good on the Sabbath' (12.11–12).

Here is a characteristic *a fortiori* argument;[16] but its conclusion is very different from Jesus' counter-question about 'doing good'. It is well known that many of the rabbis envisaged emergencies which set aside the sabbath prohibitions—in particular, when a life (even the life of an animal) was in danger.[17] Had Jesus done a 'work' for the sake of a man, comparable to one which was permitted for the sake of an animal, and been challenged for it, the argument would have been an appropriate defence. But, as we have seen, according to the synoptic accounts Jesus had performed no indictable action. It may be that we have here the recollection of a saying which was originally spoken to justify an apparently illegal action; but the author of Matthew's Gospel was evidently unaware of such an episode, and appears simply to have inserted the say-

---

[16] The rabbis called it *qal wahomer*, and used it frequently, as did Jesus.

[17] S-B I, 629. Note however that this was not permissible according to the Damascus Document, CD 11.14.

ing here because it seemed generally appropriate (whatever its original meaning and context).[18] However this may be, the testimony of the three Synoptic Gospels is unaffected: Jesus is not recorded to have performed acts on the sabbath which could have had immediate consequences at law. The case is indeed even clearer in the two additional sabbath stories recorded in Luke. In the first (the healing of a crippled woman in the synagogue) Jesus' action amounted to no more than laying his hands on the sufferer; and the ruler of the synagogue blamed the crowd as much as Jesus: they should have brought their sick on another day of the week and not on the sabbath! (Luke 13.10–17). In the second (the healing of a man with dropsy) it is not reported exactly how Jesus performed the cure; but again, there is no suggestion that his opponents sought to frame a charge against him. The picture, indeed, is quite consistent: Jesus was remembered to have effected cures on the sabbath, but not in such a way as to have broken the law. The sayings associated with these episodes are criticisms of a prevailing attitude, not reasoned defences against a charge of transgressing the Law; and the opposition which Jesus provoked on these occasions, though it is quite understandable at a human and psychological level,[19] does not appear to have been a consequence of any deliberate confrontation with the sabbath regulations.

There is, however, a saying of Jesus, preserved only in the Western text of Luke, which is of a more dangerous character (6.5D):

On the same day he saw someone working on the Sabbath, and said to him: 'Man, if you know what you are doing

[18] Many have maintained that the *Sitz im Leben* of the saying is a debate between Jewish Christians and Jews about the proper observance of the sabbath; cf. G. D. Kilpatrick, *The Origins of the Gospel according to St Matthew*, 116; Lohse, *TWNT* VII, 30, n.231. But what is the evidence for the kind of dispute to which this story would have been relevant? See above, p. 71, n.13.

[19] Which is how it is described in Luke; cf. 6.11— αὐτοὶ δὲ ἐπλήσθησαν ἀνοίας.

you are blest, but if you do not know, you are accursed and a transgressor of the law.'

The antithetic form of the saying suggests a Palestinian origin;[20] and in particular the pivotal importance of the participle 'knowing' (*eidōs*) brings it closely into relation with the sabbath regulations. By the time of the Mishnah (and doubtless much earlier), it was an established principle that an *unknowing* or accidental transgression of the sabbath was less culpable, and subject to a less severe penalty, than a deliberate one.[21] In the emphatic second half of this saying,[22] Jesus states the exact opposite: even an inadvertent transgression attracts a curse and a legal penalty; whereas a deliberate transgression, though it would also doubtless incur the risk of prosecution, might have such good reason that it would set aside the sabbath and attract God's blessing.[23] The saying could be authentic; if so it was dangerous, in that it would imply a claim by Jesus to be able to authorize an act that would be condemned by the regular courts. Such a claim, as we shall see, might have been actionable. Unfortunately the details of the episode to which it belonged have not been preserved, and we do not know whether action was taken.

Apart then from this one instance, which is of questionable authenticity,[24] the evidence of the Synoptic Gospels is consistent—Jesus performed no action on the sabbath which could have resulted in his being brought to trial, even though the acts which he did perform, and the words with which he

[20] cf. M. Black, *An Aramaic Approach* (3e.), 172, n.3.

[21] M. Sanh. 7.8; Shab. 7.1. For a striking instance of the rabbinic idiom corresponding to εἰδώς, μὴ εἰδώς cf. M. Hor. 2.1.

[22] It is characteristic of Jesus' teaching, couched in parallel clauses, that the emphasis falls on the second. cf. J. Jeremias, *N.T. Theology* I, 18; *Unknown sayings of Jesus*, 51.

[23] This principle seems to be implied also by Rom. 14.22–3.

[24] In this case, the view that the saying arises from a situation in the early Church is more plausible: Jewish Christians might occasionally feel themselves 'blest' if they set an action commanded by the Christian ethic above the observance of the sabbath prohibition. cf. Roloff, op. cit., 87f.

accompanied them, were understood to be highly provocative. This conclusion enables us to see how great is the contrast when we turn to the Fourth Gospel. There, in each of the sabbath episodes (5.1–9; 9.1–7, 14), the action authorized or performed by Jesus is one of those explicitly prohibited in the Mishnah: carrying a bed, and making a paste.[25] As we have seen,[26] the first had legal consequences; the second seems not to have done so, presumably because no authoritative witnesses were present, and a great deal of interrogation was necessary to establish the facts. Nevertheless, in both cases the evangelist is careful to emphasize the legal aspect of the matter. In the first, the statement that the erst-while cripple 'picked up his bed and began to walk about' is immediately followed by the note that 'it was the Sabbath' and by the Jews' formal warning to the man that he was transgressing it (5.9–10). That is to say, the reader is made fully aware that something has been done which is *prima facie* against the law. In the second case, the report that Jesus 'put paste on my eyes ...' elicits the immediate judgement, 'This man does not keep the Sabbath' (9.15–16). Moreover, Jesus actually refers to the first of these acts as a 'work' (*ergon*—7.21). There can be no doubt that the author of this Gospel intended Jesus' acts on the sabbath to be understood as direct and deliberate transgressions of the law, and (as we have seen) legal consequences followed.

The discrepancy here between the Fourth Gospel and the Synoptics is manifest. The fourth evangelist presents two sabbath episodes in a form which makes it quite clear that Jesus was running the risk of immediate prosecution; whereas, in the Synoptic Gospels, no illegality is proved, and the discussion involves, not the defence by Jesus of a specific action, but a criticism of the existing sabbath customs and legislation. The point in common between the two accounts is the fact that Jesus performed acts on the sabbath which aroused comment and opposition; but only in the Fourth Gospel is there any

[25] M. Shab. 10.1–5 (carrying any burden); ibid., 7.2 (kneading).
[26] Above, pp. 49f.

question of a legal prosecution. This conclusion must be borne
in mind while we consider the second of the two indictable
offences which Jesus was held to have committed.

BLASPHEMY

That Jesus claimed, or admitted, that he was the Son of
God—and that this amounted to blasphemy and was punish
able by death—is the view (as we said at the end of chapter 3)
of all the Gospels. But it is a view which causes great difficulty
among modern scholars,[27] mainly because it seems to conflict
with the rabbinic evidence. The only definition known to us
of the offence of blasphemy (M. Sanh. 7.5) makes it clear
that, for a capital offence to be established, it was necessary
for the blasphemer to have pronounced the Divine Name. This
definition depends upon a rabbinic interpretation of two verses
of Leviticus (24.15–16). The biblical text runs:

15b Whoever curses God, shall bear his sin.
16　He who blasphemes the name of the Lord shall be put
　　to death. (RSV)

In the context of the story in which they occur, these two
verses may have originally meant the same thing: the penalty
for blasphemy is death. But certain obscurities in these verses
made it possible to interpret them in a more subtle way. The
penalty prescribed in the first clause ('shall bear his sin') was
taken to mean that God would himself exact the penalty, and
the only sentence which need be imposed by a human court
was excommunication (*kareth*);[28] whereas the second clause
evidently specified an offence which carried the death penalty.
It followed that the two offences must be different; and it
suited the rabbinic tendency to reduce the number of offences
punishable by death to interpret the rather obscure Hebrew

[27] cf. the opinions cited by Hugo Mantel, *Studies in the History of
the Sanhedrin* (1962), 273–6.

[28] This, at any rate, was the interpretation given by R. Aqiba
(B. Ker. 7b); evidently the correct interpretation remained in doubt
until at least the second century A.D.

phrase[29] in the second one very precisely as 'naming the
Name'. On this interpretation, it would have been fairly difficult to commit the offence of blasphemy in such a way as to
become liable to the death penalty; Jesus' offence does not
appear to have been a case of 'naming the Name', and if this
interpretation was the normal one in the courts in the time
of Jesus, the Gospel narratives of Jesus' trial must be regarded
as implausible.

But was this the normal interpretation at the time, or even
the most common one? Some support for it may be found
in the Septuagint Greek translation of verse 16, which runs,
'He who names the name shall be put to death.' That is to
say, those who translated this somewhat obscure Hebrew
phrase into Greek in Alexandria in the second century B.C.
seem to have been ready to assume that the only type of blas-
phemy-offence which was explicitly stated to be punishable
by death was 'naming the Name'. But even on this interpretation, much would have depended on the meaning of the previous verse. The Septuagint version runs, 'He who curses God
shall bear his sin.' On the face of it, this could be taken to
mean that, whereas specifically uttering the Name was punishable by death, any other kind of cursing or blasphemy was
punishable only by excommunication (*kareth*)—and this is
precisely the view of the rabbis in later centuries. But it is
highly significant that both Philo and Josephus—who furnish
us with evidence for views held in the first century A.D. in
widely different cultural environments—take a quite different
view. Philo, for example, finds it inconceivable that any form
whatsoever of cursing or blaspheming God should not carry
the death penalty (when the less heinous offence of reviling
one's parents did so),[30] and solves the difficulty by taking the
first clause to refer to heathen gods:[31] on this view, cursing

[29] *nokev*, a word which normally means 'pierce', and may mean
anything in this context from 'blaspheme' to 'utter' (see the range
of translations in Origen's *Hexapla*).
[30] *De Vit. Mos.* II, 204.
[31] ibid., II, 205.

a heathen god made one liable to excommunication, while blaspheming the Name of the God of Israel carried the death penalty. Thus far, this interpretation was shared by Josephus, who also knew of two offences—one of cursing heathen gods[32] and the other of blaspheming the God of Israel.[33] But we are still left with the question, what did this capital offence of blaspheming consist of? Was it committed only when the Name was uttered (as the rabbis later formulated it) or did it cover any kind of blasphemous utterance? On this Philo is quite explicit. For him, 'naming the Name' means any 'unseasonable' uttering of God's name[34]—the kind of thing which is often regarded as relatively trivial, and is often done unintentionally. Yet even this is punishable by death. It follows, *a fortiori*, that any other form of blasphemy must be an equally serious offence, and must therefore attract the death penalty. The testimony of Josephus is less clear than that of Philo, but it points in the same direction. In his one reference to the law on this matter he writes: 'Let him that blasphemes God be stoned and hung for a day and buried without honour and obscurely.'[35] 'Blaspheme', in Greek as in English, is a fairly general and comprehensive word,[36] and we cannot be sure exactly what Josephus meant by it. But it seems unlikely that he would have used it if the offence he had in mind had been only the very limited and specific one of 'naming the Name'. It seems that both these authors, who belong to the same century as the writers of the Gospels, were familiar with an interpretation of Leviticus 24.16 which made any utterance punishable by death which constituted blasphemy against the God of Israel.

This evidence is by no means sufficient to establish the interpretation of the law on blasphemy which would have de-

[32] *Ant.* IV, 207; *C.A.* II, 237.

[33] *Ant.* IV, 202.

[34] *De Vit. Mos.* II, 206—ἀκαίρως φθέγξασθαι τοὔνομα.

[35] *Ant.* IV, 202.

[36] Doubtless representing the Hebrew *yᵉkallel*, on which see Derrett, *Law in the New Testament*, 454: it meant any utterance diminishing the honour of God.

termined the judgement of a court such as that which heard
the case of Jesus. But it does show that the later rabbinical one
was by no means the only one : a more rigorous one was certainly familiar to Philo and probably to Josephus. In the light
of this, it would be unreasonable to reject out of hand the
remarkably consistent testimony of the Gospels that Jesus, by
claiming or admitting that he was Messiah and Son of God,[37]
laid himself open to a charge of blasphemy that was punishable
by death. Not only do the accounts of the trial in the Synoptic
Gospels depend entirely on this assumption, but we have the
explicit statement in the Fourth Gospel, 'We have a law; and
by that law he ought to die, because he has claimed to be the
Son of God' (19.7). Moreover, there is one further piece of
evidence that this was in fact the charge on which Jesus was
convicted and sentenced to death. In Deuteronomy, there is
an injunction that the body of one who had been executed for
a capital offence should be hung on a gibbet until nightfall
(Deut. 21.22). In practice, according to both Josephus[38] and
the Mishnah,[39] this was done only in the case of a conviction
for blasphemy. Now of course Jesus was executed by the
Romans, and crucifixion was not a form of execution recognized
in Jewish law. But it bore a certain resemblance to hanging.
Consequently no fewer than three New Testament writers[40]
felt able to describe Jesus' execution in terms borrowed from
the law about 'hanging' in Deuteronomy 21.22–3. But this
form of punishment, as we have seen, was carried out only
in the case of blasphemers. It appears, then, as if both Paul
and the author of I Peter believed that Jesus had been convicted
on the one charge—blasphemy—which would have made this

[37] Or possibly by implicitly claiming the right to sit at the right
hand of God (Mark 14.62): that this would have counted as
blasphemy is a possible inference from B. Sanh. 38b. cf. W. Foerster,
TWNT III, 1088 (ET 1089); D. R. Catchpole, *The Trial of Jesus*
(1971), 140–1.

[38] *Ant.* IV, 202.

[39] Sanh. 6.4, which adds idolatry as a possible case.

[40] Paul (Gal. 3.13); the author of I Peter (2.24); and the author of
Acts (5.30 and elsewhere).

form of execution appropriate. To this extent, they offer impressive support to the evidence of the Gospels that the charge laid against Jesus in the Jewish court was that of blasphemy, and that it was on this charge that he was found guilty and condemned to death.[41]

We may now draw together the results of this chapter. All the Gospels agree that Jesus performed or permitted acts on the sabbath which provoked controversy. But in the Synoptics, these acts, though controversial, do not appear to have been illegal, nor to have had any legal consequences. In the Fourth Gospel, on the other hand, all the episodes of healing on the sabbath are clearly presented as transgressions of the law, and as providing grounds for the prosecution of Jesus. The case is similar with regard to blasphemy. All the Gospels agree that Jesus claimed or admitted that he was the Messiah, the Son of God. In the Synoptic Gospels, this admission is recorded only in the trial before Caiaphas, where it results immediately in the judicial condemnation of Jesus on a charge of blasphemy. In the Fourth Gospel, on the other hand, this claim or admission of Jesus becomes the turning-point of no fewer than five incidents, in each of which it places Jesus at the risk of immediate judgement, condemnation, and sentence at the hands of competent witnesses. In order to understand the reasons for which the author of this Gospel has presented these incidents as actual 'trials', rather than merely as points of controversy, we must now try to see what was at stake in the claims which Jesus made, and what grounds are offered on which, first his contemporaries, and then the reader, might base their verdict.

---

[41] The issue is of course complicated by the fact that $\beta\lambda\alpha\sigma\phi\eta\mu\epsilon\hat{\imath}\nu$ may be used in a non-technical sense to mean little more than 'revile' (e.g. Mark 15.29). But, apart from the trial scene, the only instance in the Synoptics which comes near enough to the technical sense to raise the possibility of legal proceedings is in the healing of the paralytic: 'He is blaspheming! Who can forgive sins but God alone?' (Mark 2.7). Yet there is no suggestion in any of the synoptic accounts that Jesus was here putting himself at risk with regard to the law.

5

The Defence

The previous chapters have established that, according to the presentation in the Fourth Gospel (and to a significantly greater degree than in the Synoptic Gospels), there were sufficient incidents in the activity of Jesus to provoke legal action against him, and that these incidents, whether or not they may be regarded as strictly historical, are used in the Gospel to provide the setting for a series of arguments in the course of which the case of Jesus is presented and examined. But this, as we observed at the beginning, is no more than a part of the matter. The Gospel is written on two levels at once. Jesus is addressing, not only his contemporary judges and prosecutors, but the reader who has to make up his own mind whether the Gospel is true. In this wider context, the issues raised by Jesus are more complex and more general than those which can be specifically defined as offences against the Jewish law. Again and again Jesus makes a statement which challenges the reader to pass judgement: if the statement is true, it demands the total assent of the believer.

Yet even if these statements by Jesus were not all immediately actionable under Jewish law, there is nothing artificial about them; they may be addressed to the reader rather than to the actual characters on the stage, yet they are entirely appropriate to their historical and dramatic context. Take the basic affirmation which, we have seen, is the crux of the whole Gospel: 'that Jesus is the Christ, the Son of God'. This is a convenient way of stating the matter, but it, too, reflects something of that artificial concentration on the Messiah question which we have seen to have been a consequence of early Christian apologetic. The question is not so much whether the evidence warrants us in using the specific title, 'Messiah', of

Jesus; but rather whether, in all that Jesus said and did, he acted as God's spokesman, as God's agent, and with God's authorization, or whether, on the contrary, his words and actions were false, blasphemous, and unauthorized. To claim that Jesus is Messiah and Son of God is of course to claim God's authorization for him. But it is not the only way of doing so, and it is necessary to take into view other claims and titles which have an equally potent implication. And not only this. We must not imagine that such questions can be raised and merely allowed to drop again if a clear answer is not forthcoming. To claim God's authorization for any word or deed is to precipitate one or other of two alternatives: either the claimant is true, in which case he must be acknowledged and obeyed; or else he is false, an agent of the devil, a blasphemer, and must be punished. Either way, a verdict must be conscientiously sought and judgement passed. Each claim demands a decision from the reader.

Perhaps the most natural and spontaneous way of expressing the conviction that someone was speaking and acting with the power and authorization of God was to call him a *prophet*. Certainly Jesus caused people to react to him in this way,[1] just as John the Baptist did;[2] and Jesus' well-authenticated use of the proverb about a prophet not being acceptable in his own country[3] suggests that he regarded the title as appropriate to himself. According to the synoptic record, this reaction was elicited by Jesus' general conduct and achievement. In the Fourth Gospel[4] (as is once the case in Luke[5]) it usually followed the performance of a particular miracle, and indeed the idea that a prophet was authenticated by supernatural signs had its roots in the Old Testament and was still accepted

[1] The crowds—Matt. 21.11; 21.46; Mark 6.15; 8.28 pars. The disciples—Luke 24.19. A Pharisee—Luke 7.39.

[2] Matt. 11.9; Luke 7.26; Mark 11.32; Matt. 14.5; Luke 20.6.

[3] Mark 6.4; Matt. 13.57; Luke 4.24; John 4.44. cf. another proverbial saying—Luke. 13.33.

[4] 4.19; 6.14; 9.17. In 7.40 it is a response to a particular utterance of Jesus.

[5] 7.16: in response to the miracle at Nain.

in Rabbinic Judaism.[6] As a response to Jesus' words and deeds, this acknowledgement that he was a 'prophet' was natural enough: it was a way of accepting Jesus as an emissary of God. Moreover, it was but a small step from this to hailing Jesus as *the* prophet—that is to say, as a person whose appearance signalled the imminence of the new age.[7] In the popular mind this distinction may not have been of much significance: the appearance of any genuine prophet would have been likely to heighten the general expectation that the new age was at hand, in which case this prophet would be readily identified with 'the prophet who is to come into the world' (John 6.14). But to the learned and responsible men of Jesus' time, the issue was more serious and more complex. As we have seen, anyone who claimed to be or admitted to being a prophet was claiming divine authorization for his words and deeds. It was assumed of course that he would hardly claim to supersede the law: rather he would be a faithful interpreter of it. But the content of his utterances and the effect of his deeds could be expected to bring something new into the situation of men attempting to live under the law, and this new factor would inevitably be a challenge to the existing authority of the scribes, who claimed to possess a tradition which guaranteed their own interpretation of the law, and doubted even the validity of a 'voice from heaven' (*bath qol*) as a source of authoritative revelation. It was doubtless this concern for the maintenance of learned authority which produced the doctrine that there had been no prophet in Israel since the close of the Old Testament period, and that there would be none until the new age began to break in.[8] It was one thing for ordinary people to acclaim Jesus as a 'prophet'. It was quite another for a learned Pharisee to concede that

[6] Siphre Deut. 18.19. cf. W. Nicol, *Semeia* (1972), 83.

[7] John 1.45; 6.14. The textual tradition wavers between προφήτης and ὁ προφήτης more than once—Luke 7.39; John 7.52. But in the last analysis the difference is not very great.

[8] cf. R. Leivestad, *Das Dogma von der Prophetenlosen Zeit*, *NTS* 19 (1973), 288–99.

Jesus, being a prophet, had therefore an authority which rendered the entire Pharisaic tradition obsolete. In order to preserve intact the respect in which the law and its interpreters were held, it was imperative to discredit the alleged prophetic status of Jesus. Once again, it is in John's Gospel that we hear most clearly the echoes of such a dispute. 'A prophet'—or 'the prophet', the difference is immaterial[9]—'does not arise from Galilee' (7.52): this is a characteristic objection of the scholar. More crude and obvious is the attack on the reputability of those who acknowledged Jesus as a prophet—the 'cursed crowd' (7.49), the man 'wholly born in sin' (9.34). It was essential to dispute Jesus' claim, if necessary by discrediting those who supported it. But again, it was not merely a question whether or not Jesus was a prophet. If he was not, then he was both sinister and culpable, a Samaritan, possessed (8.48). The choice was not between prophet and non-prophet, but between prophet and false prophet, magician, sorcerer. Significantly, these are precisely the terms of the judgement which later Judaism passed on Jesus.[10]

Another way in which it would have been fairly natural for people to acknowledge Jesus' divine commission was to recognize him as an independent and authoritative *teacher*. Again, there is good evidence in the Synoptic Gospels that this was how in fact people reacted to Jesus: they called him 'Teacher',[11] they were impressed by the authority with which he taught,[12] and Jesus' use of the proverb that the pupil is not superior to his master[13] shows that he was willing to be so

---

[9] Except in so far as it is not true that no prophet came from Galilee—witness Jonah! Those who formerly conjectured ὁ προφήτης are now found to be supported by P[66].

[10] B. Sanh. 43a, 'Jesus practised magic and misled Israel'; Justin *Dial.* 69 ταῦτα ὁρῶντες γινόμενα, φαντασίαν μαγικὴν γίνεσθαι ἔλεγον. On the schematism of true and false prophet in general, cf. K. Berger, *NTS* 20 (1973), 10, n.38.

[11] Mark 12.19, etc.; Mark 5.35; Matt. 9.11.

[12] Mark 1.27; Luke 4.32.

[13] Matt. 10.24; Luke 6.40. cf. John 13.14.

regarded.[14] But implicit in any such recognition there was, once again, a threat to the establishment. The authority of the existing interpreters of the law depended upon the conviction that they, and they alone, had access to the tradition which guaranteed the correctness and orthodoxy of their judgements. Their authority simply could not be sustained if a teacher was at large who claimed to have a direct knowledge of the will of God and whose claim found acceptance among his hearers—indeed there existed legal sanctions deliberately designed to deal with this eventuality.[15] Once again, it is in the Fourth Gospel that this issue between Jesus and his learned contemporaries is most clearly brought out. Nicodemus (himself a Pharisee, and therefore a witness who could be presumed to be fully aware of the implications) was convinced by the 'signs' performed by Jesus that he was 'a teacher come from God' (3.2); and Jesus himself is frequently made to state categorically that his teaching is not his own but derives from his Father (7.16; 8.28, 38; 14.10). This is not mere verbal hyperbole: the claim implies a real threat. As the matter is expressed in 12.47–50, 'If anyone hears my words and pays no regard to them ... [he is judged because] I do not speak on my own authority, but the Father who sent me has himself commanded me what to say ...'. This passage, indeed, contains unmistakable allusions[16] to the clause in Deuteronomy

[14] It is true that Matthew's Gospel seems deliberately to point up the picture of Jesus as teacher and of his followers as pupils (*talmidim*); but one way or another Jesus is represented as a teacher in all strands of the Gospel tradition.

[15] The case of the 'rebellious Elder', based upon Deut. 17.12. cf. M. Sanh. 11.2 and the discussion of the applicability of this to Jesus in J. Bowker, *Jesus and the Pharisees* (1973), 46–51. The possibility of such a charge against Jesus may lie behind John 18.19, cf. Dodd, *HTFG*, 95.

[16] Deut. 18.18, LXX: καὶ λαλήσει αὐτοῖς καθότι ἐντείλωμαι αὐτῷ. John 12.49: ὁ πέμψας με πατήρ, αὐτός μοι ἐντολὴν δέδωκεν τί εἴπω καὶ τί λαλήσω. Deut. 18.19: καὶ ὁ ἄνθρωπος ὃς ἐὰν μὴ ἀκούσῃ [τῶν λόγων αὐτοῦ AF] ὅσα ἐὰν λαλήσῃ ... ἐγὼ ἐκδικήσω ἐξ αὐτοῦ. John 12.47: ἐάν τίς μου ἀκούσῃ καὶ μὴ φυλάξῃ ... ἔχει τὸν κρίνοντα αὐτόν.

concerning a prophet who is to come:

> 'I will raise up for them a prophet like you ... and I will put my words into his mouth. He shall convey all my commands to them, and if anyone does not listen to the words he will speak in my name I will require satisfaction from him' (18.18–19).

These verses, as we have seen,[17] still formed the basis of an actionable offence in the time of Jesus. It is again in the Fourth Gospel that the seriousness of this claim of Jesus receives due emphasis.

So far, we have studied the issue between Jesus and his learned contemporaries mainly from the point of view of his words. But exactly the same questions are raised by certain of his deeds. 'By what authority are you doing this?' (Mark 11.28) was the inevitable and correct reaction of the scribes and Pharisees to Jesus' action in the temple. Jesus' initiative had not been sponsored or authorized by themselves, so that it must either have been illicit and punishable or else commanded by a superior authority and so have represented a threat to their own. Jesus' answer, according to the synoptic record, implicitly compared his own authority with that of John the Baptist, who had been widely acclaimed as a prophet, in which case his authority must be directly from God and so represented, once again, a threat to the scribes. This put them in a difficult situation, since for reasons given above they could hardly concede that John had been a prophet, but equally they could hardly discredit all those who had believed him to be one. Their discomfiture—characteristically for the Synoptic Gospels—brings the episode to a close, leaving the reader stunned by the brilliance of Jesus' answer. But the Fourth Gospel, once again, takes the matter further.

To understand how it does so, we need to ask what possible answer could have been given in any case. Those who asked the question believed themselves to hold all authority in such a matter. There was no way in which Jesus could claim a

[17] cf. p. 14 above.

superior authority unless either he had become the *de facto* ruler of the country or else had his authority directly from God. The first possibility is indeed mentioned: we are explicitly told that the crowd wished to make Jesus king (6.15), and the charge written on the cross itself might have suggested that Jesus spoke and acted with the authority of one who believed himself to be king—according to the Fourth Gospel it was this suspicion which ultimately proved decisive with Pilate (19.12). But the possibility is raised only to be rejected. Jesus is described as firmly declining the offer of such authority (6.15), and although the title, 'King of Israel', which was given him by Nathanael (1.49) and by the crowd at his triumphant entry into Jerusalem (12.13), was of course true in a sense, the dialogue between Jesus and Pilate (18.36–7) is carefully designed to show that it was not the sort of kingship which conferred secular authority. The true answer lay in the second alternative. Jesus' authority came directly from God.

But how was this to be expressed? Normally, a person who claimed the authority of God for any exceptional or apparently illegal act would be regarded as a rebel or a madman. The claim would carry conviction only if the person concerned could be plausibly regarded as one definitely appointed and commissioned by God to act and speak 'in his name' (5.43). The clearest analogy is from the world of commerce. No one could claim to speak or act on the authority of, say, a wealthy landowner unless he was an accredited agent whose reliability was established. Conversely, success in business depended largely on finding agents who could be trusted and relied upon to act entirely in their employer's interest.[18] Jesus might claim to be God's agent. For his claim to be accepted, his credentials would have to be established; but equally, it would be important to be able to show that he was the kind of person whom God would in fact trust as his agent. One such agent was expected: the Anointed One, the Messiah. If Jesus was

---

[18] cf. J. D. M. Derrett, *Jesus's Audience*, 76.

this agent, then his authority (as of one speaking for God) must be accepted.

We have seen that, for the purpose of convincing the reader of the Gospel, great stress is laid upon the testimony of those who recognized and acknowledged Jesus to be the Messiah and Son of God. But this is not presented merely as a matter for the reader, over the heads, as it were, of the actual characters in the story. On the contrary, the issue is energetically debated within the framework of the narrative. Even some of the crowd were ready to advance the technical objection that the Messiah would not have come from Galilee (7.27, 42), while the authorities, who could not afford to reserve judgement lest they should seem to be accepting Jesus' claim (7.26), are made to declare a ban on anyone who accepted it (9.22).[19] There were others in the crowd, on the other hand, who regarded the 'signs' performed by Jesus (about which more must be said later) as sufficient grounds for regarding him as Messiah (7.31), or who found his words so convincing that they came to the same conclusion (7.41). A debate on this very point is at the heart of the narrative in chapter 7, offering an historical precedent, so to speak, for the continuing debate in which the reader is asked to take part—whether or not Jesus is the Christ.

But there was also a more immediate and less technical way of representing Jesus as one who could plausibly be regarded as God's agent. Just as, in the world of commerce, the best agent a man would ever find would be his own son[20] (since, even apart from filial loyalty, the son's interests would be

[19] It is frequently stated that this is an anachronism. It is true that the first official condemnation of Christians dates from the time of the composition of the Gospel, not from the time of Jesus. But it does not follow that individuals who acknowledged Jesus may not have been threatened with exclusion long before that date. See the relevant evidence in S-B IV, 331 and the discussion in M.-J. Lagrange, *Jean* (2e. 1925), 266; D. R. A. Hare, *The Theme of Jewish Persecution in the Gospel according to St Matthew* (1967), 54-5.

[20] cf. Mark 12.5.

likely to coincide with his father's if he were also the heir
to his father's estate), so, in the sphere of religion, the most
reliable agent God could have would be his own Son. We
have seen that both the Synoptic Gospels and the Fourth
Gospel are evidence for the tradition that Jesus claimed to
be, and was acknowledged as, the Son of God. The original
reasons why this title was used of, and accepted by, Jesus are
still the subject of debate; but there are clear signs in the
Fourth Gospel that the evangelist saw the implications of it
as a title for God's agent *par excellence*.

Consider first Jesus' answer to the charge that he was doing
things that were unlawful on the sabbath (5.16–18). 'My
father works until now, and I am working.' From this, Jesus
is understood by his opponents (as well as by the reader) to
be referring to God as his father. But it is significant that
Jesus is not thereby claiming honour or privilege. The question here is rather, who is to be held responsible for the act
of carrying a bed on the sabbath? As we have seen, the cripple
sought to evade responsibility, since he had received an order
from Jesus. But on whose authority did Jesus give the order?
If on his own, then he was responsible and culpable. But it
was an established principle that (in cases of sacrilege, for
example) an agent could be held responsible only if he had
acted against the wishes of his employer. If he had fulfilled his
employer's instructions, then it was the employer who was
responsible.[21] In this case, Jesus' 'work' was performed by
him as God's son, God's agent, and was clearly consistent
with God's intention since God (as Jesus' opponents would
have admitted) was himself 'working' on the sabbath. Therefore, God himself was responsible: Jesus, as God's agent,
could not be charged. Jesus is made to call God his 'father'
precisely in order to establish this point. But his opponents
choose to interpret this differently: as a blasphemous attempt
to claim equality with God (5.18). Undeterred by this, Jesus
continues to develop the concept of sonship in terms of

---

[21] M. Meilah 6.1.

agency.[22] 'The son' (or 'a son') 'can do nothing on his own, unless he sees his father doing it' (5.19)—i.e. unless he knows by experience that it is the intention and the usual practice of his father. 'For what the father does, the son does in the same way' (otherwise he will be a poor agent, and may have to carry responsibility for his actions)—and the agency-model is then applied to Jesus' authority to carry out such privileged and divine acts as raising the dead and pronouncing judgement (5.21-2). Indeed, it is because the son does act as his father's agent that men must respect him exactly as they respect the father (5.23)—it was an established rule that an agent, when acting on the authority of his principal, must be treated as his principal would be if he were present.[23] Thus, throughout this dialogue, the significance of Jesus' claim to be God's 'Son' is spelled out in terms of his authority to act as God's agent.[24] Equally, it is made absolutely clear that the Jews nevertheless do not accept him as an accredited agent: 'I have come in the name of my father, and you do not accept me as such' (5.43).

This episode in chapter 5 offers perhaps the clearest instance

[22] C. H. Dodd, in a famous article (*RHPR* 42 (1962), 107–15, reprinted in *More New Testament Studies*, 30–41), saw here a 'hidden parable' of a father and his apprentice. His interpretation is not rejected here: a good agent may often need to serve first as an apprentice.

[23] For references, see p. 106, n.1 below.

[24] The smoothness of this argument is disturbed by 5.27: καὶ ἐξουσίαν ἔδωκεν αὐτῷ κρίσιν ποιεῖν, ὅτι υἱὸς ἀνθρώπου ἐστίν. Up to now, the son's authority has proceeded from the fact that he is the agent of the father. Why does it now suddenly depend on him being Son of Man? Unless (with Wendt and Bultmann) we are prepared to regard ἀνθρώπου as a secondary addition (which would certainly make the passage run more smoothly) we must assume that the idea of 'judging' has led on to the thought that this particular agent, because of his commission to judge the world, is also to be identified with the Son of Man in Daniel 7. It is this same concern with judging which seems to be responsible for the appearance of 'Son of Man' in the confession of the blind man (9.35, 39). On the implications of the anarthrous form, cf. F. H. Borsch, *The Son of Man in Myth and History* (1967), 293.

of the description of the son as God's agent. But the idea occurs frequently elsewhere: it underlies, for instance, the argument with the Jews in 7.42–7 which ends (as we have seen) in an actual condemnation of Jesus and an attempt to execute him. It is not necessary to study these instances in detail here.[25] For our present purpose, the point is gained that at least three of the titles by which Jesus was acknowledged or to which he laid claim implied an authority to speak or to act which came directly from God. Such a claim demanded immediate judicial investigation. It was necessary to examine carefully the credentials of the person who made it. We shall find that on this point also the author of the Fourth Gospel was well aware of the technical point at issue.

How could such a claim have been established? The usual way for a claimant to proceed was, of course, to summon witnesses. But we have seen that Jesus was in that rather special position, which could occasionally occur under Hebrew law, in which there were no living witnesses whom he could call upon. It is true that, in presenting the issue to the reader, the author of the Gospel is able to support Jesus' claim by appealing to the testimony of witnesses who carried undoubted authority in Christian circles and who had moreover received their information from supernatural sources. But these men could not be introduced into any episode in which Jesus' claim to be speaking and acting with God's authority was the subject of dispute between him and his contemporaries; for they were not such as to command respect in a Jewish court, and anyway, being followers of Jesus, their evidence would have been disqualified.[26] The case would of course have been different if a number of persons who carried authority or who enjoyed the general respect of society had declared in favour of Jesus. But the evangelist explicitly denies this possibility. 'Have any of the rulers (*archontes*) or of the Pharisees believed in him?'

[25] An interesting study of Jewish agency-ideas in John is made by P. Borgen in *Religions in Antiquity*, ed. J. Neusner (1968), 137–48.

[26] A probable inference from M. Sanh. 3.5; T. Demai 5.2.

is the ironical question of Jesus' adversaries (7.48); and, as if
to give an absolutely precise answer to this question, the
evangelist records later (12.42) that although many of the
rulers did believe in him, 'because of the Pharisees they did
not confess it [i.e. did not give evidence][27] lest they should be
banned from the synagogue'. That is to say, it was far from
the case that no one in authority acknowledged Jesus; but,
because of political pressure, their evidence was not forthcoming. And in any case (as we have seen) Jesus' case was
one of those exceptional ones in which no evidence, no witnesses, could have been available. The judges simply had to
make up their own minds whether or not to believe what he
said. Everything turned on the dependability of the one witness before them.[28]

Under what circumstances, then, was a witness regarded as
dependable? To some extent this was bound to depend on
the composition of the 'court' which had to decide the matter.
A group of judges who all belonged to a rigorous sect would
tend to disqualify anyone who did not observe the law with
the same thoroughness as themselves,[29] whereas a mixed group
would use other criteria. In John's Gospel, Jesus' judges use
characteristically Pharisaic language. By his attitude to the
sabbath, Jesus had shown himself to be (in their eyes) a
'sinner' (9.24) and therefore undependable. In the eyes of the
blind man who had been cured, it was equally obvious that
Jesus was 'god-fearing' (9.31) and therefore worthy of belief
(9.38). This may or may not correspond with historical reality:
the Pharisees' domination of learned disputes and legal pro-
cesses was less pronounced in Jesus' lifetime than it was when

---

[27] For the technical forensic use of ὁμολογεῖν, see especially the
papyrus evidence collected in Moulton and Milligan, *Vocabulary
of the Greek Testament*, s.v.

[28] cf. Z. W. Falk, *Introduction to the Jewish Law of the Second
Commonwealth* (1972), 115: 'The dependability of a witness is
a question that arises when there is the testimony of one witness only'.
See pp. 47–8 above.

[29] As in the Damascus Document, CD x 2–3.

the Gospel was written half a century or so later.[30] Nevertheless, it was to be expected that any group which sat in judgement upon Jesus' claims would be reluctant to accept his evidence in view of his questionable attitude to the law. It rings perfectly true, when Jesus asks, Why do you not believe me? that his judges should liken him to two persons whose evidence would be totally inadmissible in any Jewish circles —a Samaritan, or one possessed by a devil (8.48).

But there were also other, and (as we would think) less subjective criteria governing the admissibility of a witness's testimony. A generally accepted one, not only in Hebrew law[31] but in the Hellenistic world generally,[32] was that all testimony must be at first hand, and must consist of what a man has seen and heard himself. The author of the Fourth Gospel shows himself to have been well aware of this principle on a number of occasions. He who reported blood and water flowing from Jesus' side is commended as a witness precisely because he is the one who saw that to which he has testified (19.35). Similarly, the disciples are led at last to believe Jesus when they realize that he is speaking about God at first hand: 'we believe you in this case[33] because you have come from God' (16.30). Therefore it is not surprising to find that in Jesus' testimony about himself before the Jews there is much insistence on the fact that he has himself seen and heard the things which he is saying: 'We speak what we know and we give evidence about what we have seen' (3.11); 'What he has seen and heard, that is what he gives evidence about' (3.32);

[30] On the gradual development of Pharisaic rules of dependability, cf. Falk, op. cit., 123f.

[31] M. Sanh. 4.5.

[32] [Demosthenes] 46.6–7: οἱ νόμοι ... ἃ ἂν εἴδῃ τις καὶ οἷς ἂν παραγένηται πραττομένοις, ταῦτα μαρτυρεῖν κελεύουσιν. cf. also J. Beutler, s.j., *Martyria* (1972), 46.

[33] ἐν τούτῳ. cf. Moule, *Idiom Book of N.T. Greek,* 77 ('exemplary' use of ἐν); Blass-Debrunner §220 (1). There appears to be no linguistic support for the NEB rendering, 'Because of this we believe ...', which gives a *causal* sense to ἐν. The *Bible de Jérusalem* correctly translates ἐν τούτῳ 'cette fois'.

'He who sent me is true, and what I heard from him, that is
what I speak to the world' (8.26). The evangelist makes it
absolutely clear that in this respect Jesus' evidence is totally
dependable, even though (and this is characteristic Johannine
irony) his judges are unable to see how this can be so.

A further criterion of the dependability of a witness was
what we would now call the circumstantial evidence which he
could adduce in support of his claim. It is probably true to
say that, though such evidence was admissible, it carried far
less weight than we would expect it to do today. In theory
at least, the word of a dependable witness was of more significance than the production of exhibits in court or the recital
of corroborative evidence. Indeed, in capital cases such evidence was altogether inadmissible, since only 'at the mouth of
two witnesses shall he that is to die be put to death' (Deut.
17.6). A recognition of the secondary nature of such evidence
appears even in some words of Jesus in the Fourth Gospel:
'Accept the evidence of my deeds, even if you do not believe
me, so that you may recognize and know that the Father is in
me ...' (John 10.38). Nevertheless, under certain circumstances such evidence could be important and necessary. The
task of an agent provides a particularly cogent instance of this.
Consider the predicament of Tobias who was sent by his father
Tobit into a distant country, in order to recover a long-
standing debt. His task was to go as his father's agent. But
in a strange country, with no one to speak for him or certify
him, it was not likely that his word would be believed. He
therefore sensibly asked his father, 'What sign shall I give him
so that he may recognize me and believe me and give me the
money?' (Tobit 5.2).[34] If he is to be believed, an agent needs
often to be in a position to show a *sign*—which is exactly
what is demanded of Jesus after his violent activity in the

---

[34] (א) τί σημεῖον δῶ αὐτῷ καὶ ἐπιγνῶ με καὶ πιστεύσῃ μοι καὶ
δῶ μοι τὸ ἀργύριον; It is no accident that these words have almost
a 'Johannine' flavour. Rabbinic Hebrew borrowed this word from
the Greek in order to denote documentary evidence; cf. K. H. Rengstorf in *TWNT* VII, 226–7, ET VII, 228–9.

temple: 'What sign can you show us, to explain why you are
doing this?' (John 2.18). It was only to be expected that
Jesus would support his claim with evidence, and that this
evidence would take the form of 'signs'.

Indeed, there was good precedent for this. When God proposed to send Moses as his agent back to his people in Egypt,
Moses immediately sensed the difficulty he would have in
being accepted as such: 'But they will never believe me or
listen to me' (Exod. 4.11). In the following verses, God enables Moses to perform certain feats which are explicitly
called 'signs' and are intended to make the people believe
that he is indeed God's agent (Exod. 4.8–9). Not that such
signs provided fool-proof authentication of an agent: there
is a solemn warning in Deuteronomy (13.1–2) that even signs
or portents which come true must not be regarded as authen-
ticating the message of a prophet who is recommending
idolatry. Yet it was recognized that a genuine agent of God
might well be required to produce 'signs' if he were to gain
acceptance. And this recognition is clearly echoed in Paul,
who states that, with regard to the Messiah, 'the Jews demand
a sign' (1 Cor. 1.22), as indeed it is in Acts, when Jesus is
described as 'a man authenticated to you[35] by miracles and
portents and signs' (Acts 2.22). Subsequent rabbinic discussion tended to limit the admissibility of miracles as authentication of an emissary of God; but early rabbinic traditions
confirm that a miracle was legitimate evidence that a man was
God's 'agent', that is, a true prophet or (eventually) the Messiah.[36] A story told of Joshua ben Levi (*c.* 250) begins, 'By
what sign may I recognize the Messiah?'[37]

[35] $\dot{a}\pi o\delta\epsilon\delta\epsilon\iota\gamma\mu\acute{\epsilon}\nu o\nu.$ cf. Moulton & Milligan, *Vocabulary of the
Greek Testament,* s.v. $\dot{a}\pi\acute{o}\delta\epsilon\iota\xi\iota\varsigma,$ for papyrus evidence of the
forensic connotation of this word.

[36] cf. the discussion by E. Bammel, 'John did no miracle', in
Miracles, ed. C. F. D. Moule, 188–193, especially 190: 'Aqiba ...
shared the view that the miracle was evidence of the fact that the
man concerned was a prophet chosen by God.' cf. W. Nicol, *Semeia,*
80, n.1.

[37] B. Sanh. 98a.

It is against this background that we should consider the 'signs' recorded in John's Gospel. Whereas in the Synoptic Gospels the narratives of the miracles performed by Jesus normally end with a description of the amazement or excitement (or occasionally fear) of the crowds,[38] in the Fourth Gospel this feature is completely absent, and in each case the result of a miraculous incident is explicitly said to be that certain persons 'believe'[39] (or, in two cases, 'follow').[40] Moreover, as is well known, the miracles in John's Gospel (unlike the Synoptics) are called 'signs', and virtually every instance of this word 'sign', and every reference to the 'signs' performed by Jesus, is found in the context of people 'believing' (or, in one case, failing to believe) in Jesus. It is true, of course, that there is another side to this than the legal one · 'believing' in Jesus is not only a matter of accepting his credentials as an agent of God, but runs over into that 'faith' which is the basis of the Christian's relationship with his risen Lord. As always, John is speaking over the heads of his characters and has an important theological message to impart to his readers (of which 20.29, 'Blest are those who have not seen and yet have believed' is perhaps the most striking expression). Yet, for the purposes of the action in the Gospel story, the writer leaves us in no doubt, both by his treatment of the miracles and by his use of the word 'sign', of the function of these episodes in the presentation of Jesus' case: they are 'signs' which may be accepted as an important (though perhaps not the most important) part of the evidence which authenticates Jesus' claim to be speaking and acting as God's agent.

The point is expressed most clearly at the climax of the greatest 'sign' of all, the raising of Lazarus. Jesus does not need to pray aloud; but he does so expressly to show that

---

[38] For detailed references, cf. Bultmann, *History of the Synoptic Tradition*, 225–6. Many scholars believe that this is characteristic of Hellenistic rather than Jewish miracle-stories. cf. W. Nicol, op. cit., 65–6.

[39] 2.11; 4.48, 54; 11.45.

[40] 6.2; 12.18–19.

he is acting, not on his own initiative, but as God's agent: 'I spoke because of the crowd all round, so that they may believe that you sent me' (11.42). But it is also the key to the puzzling passage which follows:

> Thereupon the chief priests and the Pharisees convened a meeting of the Council. 'What action are we taking?' they said. 'This man is performing many signs. If we leave him alone like this the whole populace will believe in him....' So from that day on they decreed his death (11.47–53).

There are clear legal implications in this passage,[41] which describes an actual decision by the competent Jewish authorities.[42] The reason for their action is said to be the large number of 'signs' performed by Jesus, which could have the effect that the whole populace would believe in him. Such 'belief', as we have seen, would not have been simply a matter of religious faith: it would have meant accepting Jesus as an authoritative agent of God and therefore as the leader and ruler of the people. Such an event could well have been seen by responsible Jews as open provocation to the Roman rule, and therefore fraught with dire political consequences.

Both this treatment of the miracles and the use of the vocabulary of signs are such striking departures from the traditions preserved in the Synoptic Gospels that it is worth digressing for a moment to define the difference more precisely. With regard to the miracle stories themselves we have already observed that in the Synoptics they regularly end with a report of the amazed reactions of the crowd, whereas in John the conclusion is always in terms of 'belief' in Jesus. Yet this contrast, though striking, needs qualification. It is certainly not the case that in the Synoptics the miracle stories are told *for the sake of* their impact as miracles. On the contrary,

---

[41] Well analysed by E. Bammel in E. Bammel, ed., *The Trial of Jesus* (1970), 11ff, who also observes (33–5) that Jesus' response (vv. 53–7) is characteristic of the victim of a προγραφή.

[42] 11.53: ἐβουλεύσαντο =*consilium fecerunt.* Bammel, art. cit., 29–30.

we can see, from Mark onwards, a deliberate tendency to correct this popular emphasis and to reveal the serious purpose of the miracles. That is to say, it is by no means only the fourth evangelist who seeks to interpret as well as to narrate the miracle stories. Yet how different are the interpretations! In Mark, for example, Jesus' miraculous cures are frequently said to be the result of faith in the sufferer: in John it is belief which is the result of the miracle. Again, in Mark Jesus is credited with a desire that his miraculous cures should be known to as few people as possible: in John there is no hint of this, nor could there be, since their purpose is precisely so that people should be convinced by them of Jesus' authority. Thus all the evangelists offer an interpretation of these episodes. John differs from the others only in that his interpretation presupposes a completely different set of ideas.

With regard to the use of the word 'sign', the difference is also striking. The nearest parallel in the Synoptics to the Johannine use is in the passage where Jesus' enemies (the scribes and Pharisees, or in one case Herod) expect him to give them a 'sign'.[43] But again, what a difference! The 'sign' which is the subject of these verses is not any of Jesus' recorded miracles (for the demand comes after he has already performed many), but presumably (and we are guessing here, since close analogies fail us in either Greek or Jewish writing) the kind of absolutely decisive manifestation which would leave mankind in no doubt of the dawning of the Messiah's age. 'Signs' of this kind are familiar from the Apocalypse: they are nothing less than portents on a cosmic scale, astronomical irregularities (as in Luke 21.25) which presage the end of the world, a succession of natural disasters (precipitated, inevitably, by unprecedented astrological conjunctions) which make life barely sustainable on earth and indicate that the end is near.[44] Anxious inquiry about such alleged signs was condemned by

[43] Matt. 12.39–40; 16.1–4; Mark 8.11–12; Luke 11.16, 29.
[44] Rev. 13.13f; 16.14; 19.20. These 'signs' are also a feature of 2 Esdras, though they are not certainly so called in other apocalyptic books. cf. K. H. Rengstorf in *TWNT* VII, 230, 31ff, ET VII, 232.

the rabbis,[45] and Jesus' refusal to provide a sign, and his
strictures on those who demanded one, appear to be in the
same tradition. In the Fourth Gospel, on the other hand, none
of these connotations is present. The author has quite deliberately restricted himself to the technical meaning of 'signs'
as the kind of evidence which is admissible in order that a
man may be believed who advances a claim to be an agent.

Two further kinds of evidence were admissible in support
of a claim such as that of Jesus. Neither was strong on its own,
but they could be adduced for good measure, and both make
their appearance in John's Gospel. There was, first, the possibility of corroborative evidence in Scripture. The Mishnah
records that, in a certain dispute over the size of a house, the
fact that the temple was built according to certain proportions
laid down in Scripture was admitted as evidence as to the
proper dimensions of *any* house.[46] Similarly, Jesus makes
appeal to the fact that the Scriptures 'testify about him' and
that Moses 'wrote about him' (5.39, 46).[47] Clearly, however,
such evidence is not regarded as decisive. Secondly, the testimony of a *divine voice* was heeded in legal disputes, though
there was disagreement about its probative value.[48] A divine
voice is heard at John 12.28, answering Jesus' appeal to his
heavenly father; upon which Jesus observes that it occurred,
not for his own sake, but for that of the crowd. It is not explicitly said, but it is surely intended, that this was a *bath qol*
lending its authority to Jesus' claim to be the Son of God.

In all these ways, then, the author of the Fourth Gospel
presents the credentials for Jesus' claim to be acting and speaking with the authorization of God. It is evident at once that
his concern with this question is very much greater than that
of the Synoptic Gospels, and that the matter is argued out

---

[45] S-B IV, 1013–15.

[46] M. Baba Bathra 6.4. cf. Falk, op. cit., 117.

[47] There is a similar use of 'witness' and 'testimony' as applied
to Scripture and scriptural persons in Jubilees and 1 Enoch; cf.
J. Beutler, S.J., *Martyria* (1972), 126.

[48] Falk, op. cit., 113–14.

with a grasp of the legal implications of Jesus' claims which is unique in the New Testament. Yet here again it would be a mistake to conclude that there is no historical basis for such a presentation of Jesus. Similar material can be uncovered in the other Gospels.

We have already noted instances in the Synoptics of similar debates about Jesus. 'By what authority are you doing this?' (Mark 11.28) is the challenge uttered by the authorities after Jesus' action in the temple; whereas the crowd is prepared to recognize that Jesus' authority to teach and to heal is given to him by God (Matt. 9.8) or at least is superior to that of the scribes (Mark 1.22). Similarly, the proposition that Jesus is the Son of God is vouched for on supernatural authority[49] but is contested by Satan at the temptation (Matt. 4.6) and by the crowd at the crucifixion (Matt. 27.40) with the mocking words, 'If you are the Son of God ...', and is explicitly challenged by the judges at Jesus' trial (Mark 14.61). To these instances should probably be added the parable of the wicked husbandmen (Mark 12.1–9): the 'son' in the parable was undoubtedly an agent of his father,[50] and if Jesus told this parable in anything like its present form[51] he can hardly have done so without his hearers seeing its relevance to the question whether or not he was an accredited agent of God himself—indeed the horrified reaction ('God forbid') which they express in Luke's version (20.16) to the punishment meted out to the vinedressers is most easily explicable if one assumes that (at least in Luke's presentation) they had identified the 'son' of the parable as standing for a true 'agent' of God, in which case his murder involved also the dreadful crime of blasphemy.

But the incident in the Synoptics which comes closest to the presentation in John's Gospel is that in which Jesus is accused of carrying out his exorcisms 'by Beezebul, the prince of devils' (Matt. 12.24; cf. 9.34), and of 'having an unclean

---

[49] cf. pp. 41–3 above.
[50] cf. J. D. M. Derrett, *Law in the New Testament*, 303, 306.
[51] Which is doubted by some scholars (e.g. W. G. Kümmel, E. Schweizer) but assumed by most.

spirit' (Mark 3.30). The reality of these exorcisms was not contested by anyone. What was at stake was the identity of the power behind them. It was taken for granted that such works could not be done without supernatural aid. The question was whether Jesus was an agent of good powers or evil, of God or of the devil. There was no middle way: it must be one or the other.[52] His adversaries were bound to say that he was an agent of evil powers. The same charge turns up in John's Gospel (8.48; 10.20), and the very similar one that Jesus performed his miracles by magic continued to be voiced by the opponents of Christianity for centuries.[53] This question, indeed, is by no means peculiar to the Fourth Gospel. It is one that was raised inevitably by Jesus' activity. The critical question about Jesus was that of his authority, by whom was he sent, whom did he represent? The question is at the heart of all the Gospels. The contribution of the Fourth Gospel is to have probed so deeply into its implications.

[52] See the many instances of such arguments collected by K. Berger, *NTS* 20 (1973), 10, n.38.
[53] Justin, *Dial* 69; B. Sanh. 43a, etc.

6

The Verdict

'Christ redeemed us from the curse of the law, having become on our behalf a curse' (Gal. 3.13). Thus Paul, as we saw at the outset, acknowledges the implications of the historical facts about Jesus: he was tried by the Jewish authorities according to the law of God, and found guilty. The same acknowledgement runs through the narrative of the Fourth Gospel. Again and again, Jesus was on trial before 'the Jews', that is, before men fully competent to apply the Law of Moses to his case—and was found guilty. Indeed the verdict was never in doubt: the only historical question raised by the story is why the execution of the sentence was so long delayed. In the Fourth Gospel, a variety of reasons is given. In the Synoptics, the solution is simpler: Jesus made only one appearance in Jerusalem, and only in Jerusalem were his 'judges' powerful enough to initiate proceedings against him. But on that occasion there was no delay. Jesus was executed within a few days of his appearance. So far as the facts of the matter went, there was no room for doubt. The verdict was Guilty.

But the purpose of a Gospel, as we have seen, was to demonstrate that this was by no means the final and definitive judgement to be passed on Jesus. Jesus was the Son of God, the Messiah. Therefore the Jewish judges who condemned him were wrong. Perhaps (as the Synoptics seem to suggest) the court was corrupt and irregular, and not much notice need be taken of its verdict. Alternatively (and this is the solution of the Fourth Gospel) the law was correctly applied to the case of Jesus, but the judges failed to appreciate the force of the testimony which he produced. That is to say, those 'Jews' who, as a matter of history, had had the opportunity of passing

judgement on Jesus, were correct in their procedures but mis-
taken in their verdict.

How was the reader to be persuaded of this? First, he must
be introduced to the number and the dependability of the
witnesses who could support Jesus' claim but who, for one
reason or another, were not such as to carry weight in a trial
before 'the Jews'. We have seen that the Fourth Gospel
actually begins by calling these witnesses, and that great stress
is laid on the supernatural origin of their knowledge. Secondly,
he must hear the arguments of the parties again, but in such
a way that points that were lost on the original judges will now
come home to him. This is best done by recalling from the
Gospel tradition those episodes in which Jesus may have been
actually open to legal accusation for his words and deeds, and
rehearsing the arguments used (or likely to have been used)
by each side—making sure, however, that the reader is helped
to see the force of all the subtle allusions which his contemporaries may have missed (which is one of the ways in which
this writer's gift for irony comes into its own). These are the
episodes which occupy the central chapters of the Gospel. But
there is also a third way in which the reader may be helped
to reach the correct verdict on Jesus. He may be reminded of
all those who have subsequently 'given evidence' about Jesus,
and be told why their testimony is trustworthy. We cannot
regard the matter as settled until we have attended to the
evidence of Jesus' followers.

How were Jesus' followers prepared for this task of giving
evidence? In all the Gospels, a distinction is made between
the teaching and activity of Jesus which is fully public and
that which is intended only for the disciples. In the Fourth
Gospel, the same distinction appears, but is underlined by
the actual structure of the narrative. In the first half of the
Gospel, up to the end of chapter 12, the case of Jesus is
presented publicly. Jesus advances his claims and defends
himself before 'the Jews', his judges. Many people come to
believe in him, especially after his last great work, the raising
of Lazarus (11.45). But the verdict which has been passed

on him again and again by the Jews is 'guilty'. These chapters
have provided abundant illustrations of the astounding paradox
that 'he came unto his own, and his own received him not',
and the summary of the whole narrative thus far is that 'though
he had done such signs in their presence they did not believe
in him' (12.37).

But the next part of the Gospel (from chapter 13) has a
different function. It is concerned entirely with those who did
receive Jesus. Jesus' followers were to be the witnesses who
must now persuade men that Jesus was what he claimed to be.
These chapters show Jesus preparing his disciples for this task.
Or to put the matter in another way: the readers of the
Gospel will encounter the followers of Jesus and hear their
evidence. They will need to know how far these same
followers can be trusted as witnesses, how far they too are
'dependable'.

It is important not to oversimplify. Up to the end of chapter
12, after an initial call of the witnesses on Jesus' side, the
narrative has been a commentary mainly (but not exclusively)
on the negative statement in the Prologue: 'He came unto his
own, and his own received him not'. The initial acceptance of
Jesus by a small band of followers, the testimony of Peter on
behalf of the disciples at the end of chapter 6, the confession
of Martha before the raising of Lazarus, and the positive response of a number of anonymous individuals, are the only
favourable reactions to the claims of Jesus to set against the
repeated rejection and condemnation uttered by 'the Jews'.
But in the farewell discourses (chapters 13–17) attention shifts
to the positive side: 'To those who did receive him . . .' (1.12).
The fact of the matter is that Jesus' claims were accepted by
a small band of disciples (who are explicitly called 'his own'
in 13.1), and the discourses are concerned with the conditions
under which they will bear their testimony and the manner
of Jesus' continuing presence with them. The canvas is a large
one in these chapters, and contains many themes. But one of
these—that of the future witness of these disciples—can be
clearly distinguished.

We have seen that one of the ways in which Jesus' claim may be expressed is that he was his Father's 'agent'. The Jewish understanding of agency is well documented.[1] One principle, formulated already in the Mishnah[2] and doubtless of much earlier origin, was that in certain circumstances 'an agent may appoint an agent'. That is to say, it was not always necessary for the principal to recall an agent before appointing another in his place; an agent could be authorized to appoint his successor—this was one of the acts in which he might exercise his agency on behalf of the principal. This seems to be precisely the context in which we should understand Jesus' words, 'As you have sent me into the world, so I have sent them into the world' (17.18), words which are reiterated after the resurrection, 'As the father has sent me, so I send you' (20.21). The role of the disciples in the world will be in many respects that of Jesus himself. They are to be the agent's appointed agents.

A further absolutely basic principle of agency was that 'an agent is like the one who sent him'[3]—that is to say, he must be treated as if the principal himself were present. This principle appears frequently with reference to Jesus (5.23; 12.45), and is explicitly extended to the disciples: 'he who receives anyone whom I send receives me, and he who receives me receives him who sent me' (13.20). But this principle also has its negative side. If the agent is *not* respected, this shows that men have failed to acknowledge that he is truly an agent, or have shown disrespect to his principal. This, as we have

---

[1] cf. J. D. M. Derrett, *Law in the New Testament*, 52; P. Borgen, op. cit., (see above, p. 92, n.25) K. H. Rengstorf in *TWNT* I, 414–16, ET I. 414–16.

[2] M. Gittin 3.5–6. cf. B. Gittin 29b; Qid. 41a. This is denied by T. W. Manson, *The Church's Ministry* (1948), 36–7, who ignores the talmudic evidence. cf. L. M. Simmons, *The Talmudical Law of Agency*, *JQR* VIII (1896), 629f.

[3] Refs. in Derrett, loc. cit., to which add Mek. Exod. 12.3; 12.6; M. Ber. 5.5.

seen, is precisely what happened to Jesus: 'he who does not respect the son does not respect the father' (5.23). The Jews imagined they were merely rejecting the claims of a spurious agent: in fact they were showing disrespect to the principal, who was God himself. In exactly the same way, the disciples would receive the same disrespect and lack of acknowledgement as Jesus: they would be hated (15.18–19), persecuted, and disobeyed (15.20) just as Jesus was.

An agent's credibility did not depend entirely on his commissioning. As we have seen in the case of Jesus himself, he might be required to produce evidence of his agency. In part, this evidence took the form of 'signs'. It may have been due to a concern to emphasize the uniqueness of Jesus' 'signs' that the author of the Gospel does not use the word of anything the disciples may do. But he does allow that they will perform 'works'. He has just emphasized the importance of 'works' as a secondary type of evidence to lead men to believe Jesus' testimony (14.11; cf. 10.25); and he goes on to say that he who believes in Jesus (and so becomes a witness and an agent) will also perform the same works, 'and indeed greater works'. He adds Jesus' explanation: 'Because I go to the father'. The original agent is returning to the principal. After his return, it is for the new agents to carry on the work, and it is promised to them that they will then be able to perform such works as will provide them with effective credentials.

In all this, however, they will have powerful support, and of a very particular kind: a *paraclete*. The word occurs only in the Fourth Gospel and in 1 John. We shall find that, to understand it, we need once again to probe into the specifically Jewish mentality of the author; but we must begin with what was evidently a basic conviction shared by the first generations of Christians, and one that they traced back to a promise originally made by Jesus. They must expect to appear on trial because of their religion, both in Jewish and pagan courts; but they would find that they were not alone, and their defence would not depend only on their own ingenuity. Supernatural aid would be available to them, would tell them what to say, and lend cogency to their words. The source of this aid they (if not indeed Jesus)[4] identified as the Holy Spirit.[5] But none of the Synoptic Gospels, nor any of the other New Testament writers except the author of the Fourth Gospel, appears to develop this theme or to give further precision to this function of the Spirit.

In John's Gospel the Spirit is explicitly called the *paraclete*, which we know to have been a legal term entirely appropriate to the function we have described. But here we need, once again, to give careful study to the Jewish legal background. For, according to strict legal procedure as laid down in the Bible and elaborated by the rabbis, there was no place for an 'advocate' in the commonly accepted sense. As we have seen, everything depended on witnesses. The greater number of reputable persons a man could gather on his side to corroborate his own testimony the better; indeed, one sees in Psalm 127.5 the ideal situation of a man whose family and whose general prosperity give him confidence that in any trial his word will be accepted as of one manifestly upright and blessed by God. A person skilled in the law was called upon to be a judge, not an advocate; and the Hebrew language simply did not allow for any forensic activity other than 'testifying' or 'giving evidence'.[6] Consequently, on the fairly rare occasions on which an 'advocate' begins to be mentioned in rabbinic literature, it is hardly surprising that a word is borrowed for the purpose from the Greek language: either *synēgoros* or *paraklētos*. Even then, these words did not mean an advocate in the sense of a

---

[4] It is arguable that Luke 21.14–15, which promises supernatural aid, but makes no mention of the Spirit, is the original form of the promise; cf. C. K. Barrett, *The Holy Spirit and the Gospel Tradition* (1947), 131–2. But this is not the usual view; cf. H. Conzelmann, *The Theology of St Luke* (ET 1960), 226, n.1.

[5] There is virtually no precedent for this function of the Holy Spirit in Jewish writings; but oddly enough this has caused less surprise among scholars than the lack of Jewish precedents for what is said about the Spirit in John's Gospel.

[6] The root *'ad* covered them all. cf. B. Gemser, *Suppl., VT* III, (1955), 130, n.1.

lawyer. They meant rather a man who would appear in court
to lend the weight of his influence and prestige to the case óf
his friend, to convince the judges of his probity, and to seek
to secure a favourable verdict.[7] For obvious reasons strict
jurists were anxious to discourage the practice[8] (for it can
hardly have contributed to the impartiality of the courts!).
But we can infer, even from these negative comments upon
it,[9] that the institution certainly existed in the first century
A.D., doubtless having entered the Jewish courts from the
pagan courts which existed alongside them.[10]

Now it is highly significant that almost all the occurrences
of such an 'advocate' in rabbinic writings refer, not to actual
court proceedings on earth, but to an imagined trial and
judgement before God. That is to say, the 'advocate', who had
no proper place in correct procedure according to the Jewish
law, nevertheless provided a valuable earthly model for one
of the necessary actors in the heavenly drama of the judgement
before God. For here, however much the procedure might
be imagined to follow the normal pattern of an earthly court,
certain conditions would be very different. In particular, it
could hardly be left to the human defendant to choose 'witnesses' who could appear and testify for him: for what man
can stand before the judgement seat of God?[11] On the other
hand, it had come to be believed that there would be an
'adversary' or 'accuser',[12] who would recall before God the
individual's (or the nation's) sins. It followed that there must
be someone or something who would be admitted to God's
presence to speak on the defendant's behalf. The rabbis sug-

[7] Instances are collected by S. Krauss, *Gr.Lohnwörter* (1898) I,
210; II, 496.
[8] B. Sheb. 31a; cf. Falk, op. cit., 101.
[9] To which may be added one explicit reference: Gen. R. 18.33.
[10] So Mowinckel, *ZNW* 32 (1933), 103.
[11] The point is vividly made in 2 Esdras 7.104–5; cf. 2 Enoch 53.1.
[12] The name of this character, if not Satan himself (as in Zech. 3.1),
was also borrowed from the Greek language: κατήγορος, *qatēgor*;
cf. Mowinckel, loc. cit.

gested such notions as the person's 'good deeds' to be his
'advocate' (*paraclete*).[13] More popular writing (such as apocalyptic) introduced figures who were in any case believed to
have access to the heavenly court, such as angels[14] or Enoch[15]
or the perfectly righteous,[16] to perform a similar function.
Indeed, the notion of an advocate for the righteous when they
come to be tried before God is well attested in Jewish literature
in the New Testament period, even though no specific title
was attached to such a person.[17]

In other respects, however, the familiar procedure of the
earthly Jewish court does apply to the heavenly. In particular,
the defendant (now represented by his advocate), in meeting
the accusations of his adversary, may become the accuser:
demonstrating the righteous man's innocence may involve
convicting the accuser of falsehood.[18] Indeed, once the idea of
an 'advocate' in heaven is accepted, a large number of possible
functions converge in him. His basic task is to speak and
persuade, and so he must be eloquent. But not only does he
speak to God, the judge, and seek to persuade him of the
goodness of his friend (the function which comes nearest to
the modern understanding of 'advocacy'). He also speaks to
the accuser, in which case his speaking takes the form of
counter-accusation; and thirdly he may speak to his friend
himself, urging him to live worthily of the defence being made
for him, and helping him to understand the will of God which
he must at all costs observe.[19] A single Hebrew word was

[13] M. Aboth 4.11. Other instances in S-B II, 586. Philo also uses
παράκλητος in this sense—*Praem.*, 166.
[14] Zech. 3.4; 1 Enoch 9.1; 40; T. Dan 6.2.
[15] 1 Enoch 13—14.
[16] 1 Enoch 39.
[17] Though Enoch is called a 'witness' already in Jubilees (4.18, 22).
[18] An instance of this may be seen in John 5.45: Moses, usually
regarded as the Jews' advocate, has become their accuser! cf. T.
F. Glasson, *Moses in the Fourth Gospel* (1963), 104f. Compare also
the rabbinic saying, 'Woe to him whose advocate turns accuser!'
[19] The classic example of this function is given by the angel-
advocate in Zech. 3.7.

capable of expressing all these functions;[20] but many of them were included also under a Greek word (*elenchein*) which is familiar from John's Gospel (He will *accuse* the world'—16.8) and which was understood to cover most of the normal functions of an advocate. And the various figures whom we encounter in the heavenly court—angels, spirits, 'intercessors' such as Abraham or Enoch, and even on occasion the Holy Spirit—tend to move easily from one function to another, and there is no attempt to define or limit the exact function of each.

It need cause no surprise that Christians, who inherited and preserved from the Jewish religion a vivid concept of Judgement, should have occasionally expressed their new faith in the saving activity of Christ in terms of his advocacy before the judgement-seat of God. 'If any man sins, we have a *paraclete* in the presence of the Father ...' (1 John 2.1).[21] Such language is entirely in line with the developments we have been considering. The only novelty—and it is of course a radical one—is that it is now Jesus Christ who performs this role in heaven. Startlingly different, however, is the use of this imagery in St John's Gospel. Not 'we have a *paraclete*' (in heaven), but, 'the Father ... will give you a *paraclete* to be with you' (on earth—14.16; cf. 14.26—'the holy spirit whom the father will *send*'). As so often, this writer takes concepts and images which belong traditionally to the world to come and boldly applies them to the world of the present. For him, the *paraclete* is an advocate, not (or not only) in heaven, but on earth—providing the advocacy, in other words, which Christians have already experienced and attributed to the Holy Spirit.

It follows that it is not so much John's use of the word

[20] *litz*, on which see H. N. Richardson, *VT* 5 (1955), 169. Accordingly m*e*litz, usually translated 'interpreter', is a 'speaker of considerable fluency, but not an interpreter in the strict sense of the word' (Richardson, ibid.). m*e*litz is translated *paraclete* in Targum Job 33.23.

[21] The idea is not of course found only in the Johannine writings. cf. Rom. 8.34; Heb. 7.25.

paraclete which is arresting, as his application of the concept to the continuing 'trial' of Jesus and his disciples on earth. He was not the first or only writer to conceive of this advocate as 'the spirit': St Paul had already done so in Romans ('The spirit intercedes for the saints before God'—8.27), and the 'spirit' who speaks to the churches in the early chapters of Revelation is clearly another example of the advocate-accuser in the heavenly court. Moreover there are similar notions in independent Jewish writings.[22] Nor is it surprising that this *paraclete* should also be described as one who 'teaches' those whom he represents (14.26), 'reminds' them of instructions already given, and 'leads' them into all truth (16.13); as we have seen, this activity was a natural corollary of the function of the heavenly 'advocate'. The originality comes when this *paraclete* leaves, so to speak, the heavenly court and is 'sent' to appear on behalf of the disciples on earth. It will be as well to take these remaining *paraclete*-sayings one by one.

1. 'The *paraclete*.... the spirit of truth ... will give evidence about me' (15.26). This is the standard and most comprehensive activity of any advocate—to bear witness, or give evidence.[23] But instead of giving favourable evidence about the followers of Jesus in the heavenly court (which is the function of the *paraclete* in 1 John 2.1) this *paraclete* will give evidence about Jesus in the earthly court—as is made absolutely clear by the following sentence: 'And you give evidence, because you have been with me from the beginning' (15.27). The *paraclete* and the disciples each have the same function: to be witnesses.[24] The dependability of the *paraclete* derives from the fact that he is sent straight from God; of the

[22] T. Judah 20.5 τὸ πνεῦμα τῆς ἀληθείας κατηγορεῖ (v.l. μαρτυρεῖ πάντα καὶ κατηγορεῖ) πάντων —though this is not the heavenly court. R. Aha (3rd century) describes the Holy Spirit as *synēgor*, i.e. an advocate who also becomes an accuser (Lev. R. 6.109a). cf. S-B II, 138, 562.

[23] cf. Mowinckel, art. cit., 103.

[24] The same proposition (that both the Holy Spirit and the disciples are witnesses) is explicitly stated at Acts 5.32.

disciples, that they have been eyewitnesses—have known it all at first hand—'from the beginning'. The 'court' is any occasion when Jesus' claim to be Son of God and Messiah is denied by the enemies of the Christian community.

2. 'He will accuse the world on the grounds of sin and of justice and of judgement' (16.8). The word for 'accuse' is an almost technical one:[25] it describes the activity of the advocate when (so to speak) he passes to the attack. 'Convict' (NEB) is not a correct translation here; for the advocate is not judging. Rather he is laying accusations; and this gives the clue to understanding the following phrases. These are introduced by an ambiguous Greek particle (*hoti*) which can mean either 'that' or 'because'. But we are told that the advocate is about to launch accusations; so we expect to be told, not *why* he does so, but what the content of the accusations will be. So understood, the meaning of these difficult verses can be rendered as follows:

a 'He will accuse the world of sin, [arguing] that they do not believe in me.' The sinfulness of failing to acknowledge that Jesus was sent by God is emphasized a few verses earlier (15.21–2). Therefore to accuse someone of not believing in Jesus is to accuse him of sin.

b 'He will accuse the world with regard to [its conception and execution of] justice, saying that I go to my father and you see me no longer.' In the eyes of the world Jesus was unjust, a transgressor of the law, and received the appropriate punishment: death. Such a death, inflicted in accordance with the Jewish law, would normally be held to have been in accordance with God's will and an expression of God's justice. But Jesus' death was in fact the means by which he returned to his father. Because of the resurrection, this death was a sign, not of God's condemnation, but of God's vindication. By testifying to this, the spirit would pass to the attack against Jesus' earthly accusers, and accuse them

[25] ἐλέγχειν, representing the Hebrew *hokiah*. cf. S. Mowinckel, art. cit., 105.

in turn of having misinterpreted Jesus' death. Had this
death been what it seemed to the world, it would have been
an expression of the world's conception of justice. But in
fact it was vindication, an expression of God's true justice.[26]

c 'He will accuse the world with regard to [the issue of this
particular] judgement, showing that the ruler of this world
is [the one who has been] judged.' The judgement passed
on Jesus was 'guilty'; but Jesus had called God to witness,
which meant (as we have seen) that the tables might be
turned. His oath was true, and those who had disbelieved
him (who of course were only representative figures: behind them stood the demonic 'ruler of this world') were
themselves judged guilty.

3. 'The Father ... will give you another *paraclete*.' It would
be a mistake, as we have seen, to use the fact that Jesus is called
a *paraclete* in 1 John to prove that the sense here is 'another
paraclete like Jesus'; for in 1 John the use of the word is
different from that in the Gospel. Nevertheless, the natural
run of the paragraph suggests that this is what is meant. (By
comparison, the other possible sense, 'He will give you a
paraclete other than any you have had before', is somewhat
forced). In what sense, then, was Jesus himself a *paraclete*?
Since there is no place here whatever for an allusion to the
judgement in heaven, we must suppose that the 'trial' of Jesus'
followers is still in mind, and that the thought is a perfectly
simple one: if Jesus were still to be with his disciples when
they came under attack, they would obviously have a stupendous advocate; but he will not be present; instead, they will
have another *paraclete*, the spirit.

In all this, the evangelist is clearly building upon the fundamental Christian conviction that a follower of Jesus, when
under attack because of his faith, can expect the Holy Spirit
to come to his defence. But he has developed this beyond any

---

[26] cf. 1 Tim. 3.16—ἐδικαιώθη ἐν πνεύματι: the phrase could well
reflect a similar understanding of the spirit as the successful advocate
by whom (ἐν) Jesus was vindicated.

other New Testament writer. Any particular occasion on which a disciple is actually brought to trial is only an instance and a continuation of that eternal 'trial' in which, first Jesus, and then his followers, are inevitably involved before the judgement of the world. This, indeed, is John's radical reinterpretation of the conventional mythology of the last judgement. Jesus—and Christianity—is on trial before the world, which means also that the world is on trial before Jesus. To this trial, the language traditionally used of the heavenly court is appropriate. In particular, the inevitable figure of an advocate —a *paraclete*—can be shown also to be already active on earth, in the person of the Holy Spirit, defending and accusing. And these activities the spirit combines with others already experienced in the Christian Church (and partly understood already in Judaism) such as guiding, teaching, inspiring, and foretelling: for did not other heavenly 'advocates', such as Enoch, have the same reputation? Indeed, words are used to describe the Spirit in John's Gospel which would have been perfectly appropriate to any privileged hero or angel of the conventional apocalyptic drama: 'When he comes who is the Spirit of truth, he will guide you into all the truth; for he will not speak on his own authority, but will tell only what he hears; and he will make known to you the things that are coming' (16.13).

We must now ask whether this understanding of the followers of Jesus as his 'agents' and 'witnesses', and of the spirit as an advocate, is peculiar to the Fourth Gospel, or whether there are signs of it in other parts of the New Testament. We may begin with the verse in the Fourth Gospel (13.16) in which Jesus says to his disciples, 'A servant is not greater than his master, nor an *apostolos* than the man who sent him.' This is the only occasion on which the word *apostolos* occurs in the Fourth Gospel. It is true that the first followers of Jesus had been generally known as 'apostles' for half a century by the time this Gospel was written, and that the Christian reader, coming across this word here, would naturally think of it as a technical Christian term. Yet the

fact that this writer never uses the word elsewhere, and the
fact also that the whole point of the saying lies in its appeal
to well-known examples of the relationship of greater to less
(as of master to slave), suggest that we ought here to take
apostolos in the sense of a legal and commercial institution
well known to the Jews: 'an agent'.[27] That is to say: it was
as natural to think of Jesus' followers as his 'agents' as it was
to think of them as his 'servants'. Now it is true there are
similar sayings recorded in the Synoptics which liken the
relationship between Jesus and his followers to that between
a master and his slave,[28] or between a teacher and his pupil,[29]
but that only in the Fourth Gospel do we find the analogy
of the principal and his agent. On the other hand, we cannot
ignore the fact that from very early times these same followers
were known as 'apostles'. Why did the early Church choose
this title for the first and most authoritative of Jesus' disciples?
The reasons are no less mysterious in this case than in those
of the titles of other Christian ministers such as bishops and
deacons;[30] but the most likely origin is still that which was
suggested some forty years ago,[31] namely the Jewish institution of the 'agent', who (as subsequent legal formulations expressed it) represented his principal and must be respected
as his principal would be if he were present. The idea of such
an agent was already familiar in religious affairs, and was

[27] See p. 88 above.
[28] Matt. 10.24-5.
[29] Luke 6.40.
[30] cf. A. E. Harvey, 'Elders', in *JTS* 25 (1974), 318.
[31] By K. H. Rengstorf, *Apostolat and Predigtamt* (1934) and in
TWNT I, 414-15 (ET I, 415). This has been called into question,
e.g. by W. Schmithals, *Das Kirchliche Apostelamt* (1961), 95-9.
The objection seems to assume that what is being proposed is the
existence of a Jewish *institution* which may have served as a model
for the Christian apostolate; and this is indeed doubtful. But in
fact what is being proposed is that the legal recognition of 'agency'
in the oriental world provided the starting-point (and the title) for
the Christian idea of the 'apostle'—which subsequently of course
developed in quite different ways.

capable of many applications.[32] The basic concept was that of the authorization of an emissary in a way which would have weight (if necessary) in a court of law. This emphasis on authorization was at least a part of what the Church meant by the word when it singled out some of Jesus' first followers as 'apostles' (it is very prominent in Paul's arguments for his own apostleship). If it was led to choose the word *apostle* (*shaliach*, agent) for this reason, then its thinking was not far from that of the author of the Fourth Gospel (and—who knows?—of Jesus himself).[33]

We have seen[34] that a fundamental principle of 'agency' was that an agent was like the one who sent him, and that this is clearly expressed in John 13.20: 'He who accepts anyone whom I send accepts me, and he who accepts me accepts him who sent me.' This saying has a very close parallel in Matthew 10.40: 'He who receives you, receives me, and he who receives me, receives him who sent me', and the same idea is present in three other synoptic passages.[35] We can hardly resist the conclusion that this way of conceiving the relationship of Jesus to his disciples was known to the authors of these Gospels— was indeed implicit in certain sayings of Jesus himself, even if it is only in the Fourth Gospel that it is fully explored and substantiated.

With regard to the disciples as 'witnesses', the situation is somewhat different. We noticed earlier that the Synoptic Gospels, though they share a certain concern for the supernatural origin of the disciples' knowledge about Jesus, nowhere describe these disciples as 'witnesses', nor do they show any interest in this aspect of their future role. To this extent, the Johannine insistence upon their 'testimony' is exceptional in

[32] There is a striking religious application of it in 2 Enoch 44: 'He that brings into contempt the face of man, brings the Lord's face into contempt': man is God's 'agent'.

[33] The idea is certainly present also in Matt. 10.1: the principal gives authority to his agents to cast out devils.

[34] See p. 106 above.

[35] Mark 9.37; Luke 9.48; 10.16. On the relationships between these verses, cf. Dodd, *HTFG*, 343–7.

the entire Gospel tradition. Yet with the Acts of the Apostles (foreshadowed in this respect by one verse at the end of Luke's Gospel—24.48) we suddenly find the situation reversed: the concept of a follower of Jesus 'giving evidence' becomes relatively common.[36] Moreover, the concept of the Christian witness who by his death or suffering becomes a 'martyr', which first occurs explicitly in the Book of Revelation, was very soon to make tremendous progress in the Church. There is little evidence for the idea earlier than John's Gospel; but it seems hardly likely that so influential an idea began only there.

What then of the *paraclete*? Is the advocacy of the Holy Spirit (in the sense we have been examining) a new contribution of the Fourth Gospel? To some extent this question has already been answered by reference to those passages in the Synoptic Gospels which promise the help of the spirit to Christians appearing in court for their faith. That Christians would have to 'bear witness', and that they would never be alone when doing so, was a universal conviction in the early Church, and is formulated in a number of different ways.[37] What is new in John's Gospel seems to be the conception of this advocate passing to the attack. This is the moment to bring into view a further passage from the Fourth Gospel:

'Saying this he breathed upon them and said, Accept the Holy Spirit; if you remit anyone's sins, they are remitted; if you retain their sins, they are retained' (20.23).

The most natural meaning of these words would appear to be on the lines of the charge given to Peter in Matthew 16; but in this case the Holy Spirit would seem to have a function nowhere else even hinted at in this Gospel: the exercise of

---

[36] Acts 1.8; 2.32; 4.33 and at least nine other instances. Note especially Acts 5.32 in comparison with John 15.26–7.

[37] Mark 13.9–11; Matt. 10.17–20; Luke 12.11–12; 21.13–15; Acts 7.55; 1 Cor. 12.3. cf. Dodd, *HTFG*, 411: the promise was 'so deeply rooted in the oral tradition that it appeared in several different branches of that tradition, taking slightly different forms'.

discipline over the Christian community. A meaning much more appropriate to the context (which is that of 'sending out' the disciples, commissioning them as agents) is obtained if we keep in mind the function of the Holy Spirit as *paraclete*, meeting the attacks of the world with counter-accusations. As was said in 16.9, the spirit in this role was to accuse the world of sin; and since witness and judge were one, its accusation would amount to condemnation. It follows that the disciples, accepting such advocacy on their behalf, would have the power to convict their enemies or to forgive them.[38] Now this saying is certainly related to the charge given to the disciples in Matthew 18.18, 'Whatever you bind on earth will be bound in heaven, and whatever you loose on earth shall be loosed in heaven'. The form in Matthew is most easily explained in terms of synagogue discipline, the forbidding or permitting of certain interpretations of the law, or the excommunication or readmission of members. The Fourth Gospel seems to have applied a similar saying in a different sense. But that sense too is widely shared; for was it not firmly believed, and on Jesus' authority, that Christians were to judge the world? (Matt. 19.28; Luke 22.30; 1 Cor. 6.2).

It may be in fact that the closest point of contact between the Johannine *paraclete* and the Spirit in the synoptic tradition is to be found in the difficult saying in Mark 3.28-9:

I tell you this: no sin, no slander, is beyond forgiveness for men; but whosoever slanders the Holy Spirit can never be forgiven; he is guilty of eternal sin.

There is, first, a clear biblical background to this saying. The one offence for which it was stated in the Torah that God would give no forgiveness and accept no satisfaction was 'taking his name in vain' (Exod. 20.7)—a commentary on this may be read in Ecclesiasticus 23.10, 'the man who has oaths and the sacred name for ever on his lips will never be clear

---

[38] cf. the interpretation offered of these verses by B. Lindars, *The Gospel of John* (1972), 612-13.

of guilt'.[39] Even if it was the case that human courts became
reluctant to impose the death penalty for blasphemy,[40] no one
doubted that God would exact his own penalty for it. An
extension of this was found in Exodus 23.20–1: 'I send an
angel before you.... Take heed of him and listen to his voice.
Do not defy him; he will not pardon your rebelliousness, for
my authority rests in him.' That is to say: the Old Testament
recognized one unforgivable sin—blasphemy—and envisaged
this sin being committed if blasphemous words were used
against an authorized agent of God.

Against this background, it can be seen at once that the
real force of Jesus' saying lies in its first clause: God forgives
every slander, every sin! Yet even Jesus' proclamation of the
forgiving grace of God does not repeal the one law in the
Torah for which no forgiveness is possible. Now all this is
very close to the thought of the Fourth Gospel. The world
does not accept the claims of Jesus. If Jesus had been a false
claimant, then the world would have judged him, and would
correctly have condemned him to death. But as Jesus' claims
are true, it is the world that is judged: 'You will die in your
sins' (8.21), 'Your sin remains' (9.41). The sin of refusing to
accept Jesus—which (since Jesus is God's authorized envoy)
is blasphemy—is as final and unforgivable as it is in the saying
in Mark,[41] and indeed as it was bound to seem to any Christian
brought up in the law of the Old Testament.

But the saying we are concerned with defines this sin as
'blasphemy against the Holy Spirit'. The brief commentary
added by Mark (but not by Matthew), 'it was because they
said that he had an unclean spirit', is correct in so far as it
places the unforgivable sin in the context of judgement about
Jesus—was he sent by God or the devil, was he a prophet or

[39] cf. Philo. *Spec. Leg.* II, 253, who confirms the seriousness of
the crime, but understands it in the limited sense of a perjurious
oath, as does Josephus (*Ant.* III, 91).

[40] see pp. 77–8 above.

[41] But the Q version adds that blasphemy against the Son of Man
(as opposed to the Spirit) *is* forgivable (Matt. 12.38; Luke 12.10).

a magician? But it is probably not correct in so far as it refers the matter to an act of exorcism by Jesus. The spirit whom the world blasphemes is the spirit which the Christians have as their advocate in the great and continuing 'trial' of Jesus before the world. It (like the disciples—John 15.26) 'bears witness' for Jesus; and since the world cannot 'accept' its evidence (14.17), the world necessarily stands convicted of the unforgivable sin. The presuppositions underlying the saying in Mark and Matthew and the Johannine presentation of the *paraclete* are the same.[42]

But there is one further feature of this *paraclete* which takes us back to the underlying paradox of the Gospel. He is one 'whom the world cannot accept, because it neither sees him nor knows him' (14.17). The disciples are to receive the help of this tremendous advocate when they give their testimony before the world—but it will not be acknowledged! 'He came unto his own and his own received him not'—the same conditions continue to apply when the case of Jesus is presented by his followers. Even with the *paraclete* on their side they may not be believed. The reader, when he encounters this powerful witness, must not expect to be swept off his feet. The paradox, envisaged already in the servant songs of Second Isaiah, still obtains:[43] God may appoint and authorize witnesses to the truth, but their evidence may not be accepted. In the last analysis it is still the reader or the hearer who has to make up his mind whether Jesus is the Messiah, the Son of God.

It was the task of the Gospel writers to present the case of Jesus Christ. We have seen how the author of the Fourth

[42] The same understanding of 'blasphemy against the Holy Spirit' underlies the addition made in the Koine text to 1 Pet. 4.14: ($\kappa\alpha\tau\grave{\alpha}$ $\mu\grave{\epsilon}\nu$ $\alpha\mathring{v}\tauo\grave{v}s$ $\beta\lambda\alpha\sigma\phi\eta\mu\epsilon\hat{\iota}\tau\alpha\iota$, $\kappa\alpha\tau\grave{\alpha}$ $\delta\grave{\epsilon}$ $\mathring{v}\mu\hat{\alpha}s$ $\deltao\xi\acute{\alpha}\zeta\epsilon\tau\alpha\iota$) of which the context is a Christian under attack for his faith. More common, however, is the identification of the Holy Spirit in the Marcan saying with the spirit of prophecy: *Didache* 11.7; Acts 7.51–2.

[43] For a recent study of this theme, see O. Michel, *Zeuge und Zeugnis* in *Neues Testament und Geschichte* (Cullmann Festschrift, 1972), 15–31.

Gospel accomplishes this task with particular sharpness and expertise, exploiting as none of the others did those occasions and issues which placed Jesus on trial before those of his contemporaries who were competent to judge him. But it is in the nature of the case that no evidence can be decisive, no evidence is unassailable. The case is still open, the trial is still on. No one can pronounce the verdict for us: each of us has to determine it for himself.

POSTSCRIPT:

The Record of the Proceedings

The argument of the preceding chapters has moved forward with a certain momentum of its own. The hypothesis that the literary form of a trial, conceived according to Jewish conventions and procedures, can throw light on the composition of the Fourth Gospel has been applied to some characteristic passages and has been found fruitful. The evangelist's task was to persuade men to believe that 'Jesus is the Christ, the Son of God'. To accomplish this, he appears to have cast much of his material in the form of a long-drawn-out trial, in which the underlying issues are exposed and by which the reader is challenged to form his own judgement and cast his own verdict. The progress of the drama, the construction of the dialogues, and even the terminology of the debate, have all become clearer in the light of this legal model—a model which perhaps needed such painstaking reconstruction only because the legal procedures which it presupposes were significantly different from those of the western world and have therefore lost their power to offer a significant intellectual framework to the modern reader.

It remains only to indicate the implications which the correctness of this hypothesis might have for the study of the Gospel as a whole. It must be said at once that in relation to the richness of ideas in the Fourth Gospel the hypothesis is of modest scope. The Gospel has a complex texture, and we have sought to distinguish only a single strand. If it is true that the evangelist was concerned to present the case for Jesus under the form of a trial, then this was only one of the things he was concerned to do. Any conclusions which may be drawn from this study must be reconciled and combined

123

with the many other interests which may be believed to have influenced the author. Yet one cannot believe one has detected even one of the motives which made him write as he did without thereby forming some judgement about the coherence of his work as a whole. The Gospel as we now possess it has often given the impression of erratic composition or disorderly editing: some parts seem not to follow well upon others and evidence has occasionally been assembled from its pages of such apparent contradiction between one passage and another that commentators have felt bound to assume the presence of more than one hand in its composition, or at least of an imperfect stitching together of previously existing material. Doubtless the case for such disturbance and imperfection is still strong, and in certain sections is unaffected by our argument. But the proposed legal model has at least given a new measure of coherence to the composition of some passages (in particular the prologue and the calling of witnesses in the first chapter) and has offered a solution to at least one apparent inconsistency (the question of the validity of a single witness in 5.31 and 8.14). If it is accepted, it removes certain objections to regarding the Gospel, in the form in which we possess it, as the finished work of a single author, and so strengthens the case of any critic who, on other grounds, wishes to argue that the Gospel comes to us substantially in the form which the writer originally intended.

There are, however, three questions in the contemporary debate about the Fourth Gospel to which our hypothesis is capable of making a weightier contribution. These questions concern, first, the historicity of the words and deeds attributed to Jesus in this Gospel; secondly, the milieu in which the Gospel was written and in which the author was educated; and thirdly, the object of the Gospel and the type of reader for whom it was written. It will be as well to take these three questions separately.

1. *Historicity* Recent study has tended to narrow the gap which, since the beginning of modern critical scholarship, has

been assumed to exist between the relatively faithful reporting of the Synoptic Gospels and the apparently free and discursive narrative of the Fourth. It has been demonstrated that the author of John's Gospel had access to sources of information other than the Synoptic Gospels, and that these sources may have preserved material which is as old and as reliable as anything which was available to the Synoptics. Moreover, the treatment of this material in the Fourth Gospel has been found to be subject to the control of historical considerations to a greater degree than was formerly supposed; and in the meantime the Synoptic Gospels themselves have been seen less and less as simple records of fact and more and more as sophisticated theological interpretations of the received oral tradition. At the risk of oversimplification, it could be said that in the past the picture of Jesus as presented in the Synoptics was thought of as a photograph taken from slightly different angles, while that in the Fourth Gospel appeared to be a free portrait by a painter with a markedly individual style. Today it is nearer the truth to think of the synoptic narratives as the creations of individual artists (subject, of course, to the control of a strict convention) and of the author of the Fourth Gospel as working on a similar likeness with not altogether dissimilar methods.

The present study has tended to endorse and corroborate this tendency. The apparently distinctive presentation of John the Baptist and the first disciples as 'witnesses' has been found to have at least an echo in the Synoptics, and moreover to be compatible with them; the treatment of 'Son of God' and 'Messiah' in each has been shown to have important similarities; the basic data for our understanding of the work of the Holy Spirit have been identified as common to all the Gospels; and even the narratives of the trial of Jesus, which seem at first sight to represent widely different versions of the facts, have turned out to come close to each other in many points of detail. So far as general historicity is concerned, the gap between the Synoptics and the Fourth Gospel may be said to have been reduced still further by some of our conclusions.

This does not mean, of course, that the gap could ever be altogether closed. To take only one example: the sayings of Jesus, as recorded in the Synoptics, are pithy, concise, and highly memorable. It is not difficult to see how sayings of this kind could have been preserved in people's memories until they came to be written down, and a good case can be made out for a large number of them being reasonably faithful reproductions of authentic sayings of Jesus. But how different is the situation in the Fourth Gospel! There the words of Jesus are reported in the form of long and close-knit speeches. Admittedly, one can detect ideas and motifs and sometimes even whole phrases which have parallels in the Synoptics, and it is perfectly plausible to argue that the Johannine discourses, are, in their own idiom, a faithful representation of Jesus' meaning. But it is inconceivable that such complex literary units could ever have been memorized and preserved in oral tradition. As an *historical* record of what Jesus actually said, they cannot be compared with the material collated in the first three Gospels.

Yet again this contrast must not be overdrawn. We have identified a literary form which may well have influenced the fourth evangelist's presentation of some of the episodes in the life of Jesus and of the dialogues associated with them: that of the law-suit, or *ribh*. The presence of such a literary influence may seem to result in a corresponding reduction of historical reliability. But this is by no means the only such literary form which has been detected in the Gospels. Consider the apocalyptic discourse in Mark 13, and the corresponding chapters in Matthew and Luke. These are undoubtedly literary compositions (Mark 13.14), and it is highly unlikely that Jesus gave his teaching in precisely this form. Yet few would doubt that there was, at the very least, an apocalyptic ingredient in Jesus' understanding of history, and that he is therefore likely to have made use of apocalyptic imagery and conventions in order to convey his meaning.[1] Mark 13 is not

[1] The Mishnah (Sotah 9.15) records the reaching of a first-century rabbi cast in a similar 'apocalyptic' form.

usually thought of as altogether unhistorical. Similarly with the Fourth Gospel. The dialogues between Jesus and his Jewish adversaries are undoubtedly literary compositions. Yet there is no reason to doubt that Jesus was in fact involved in legal disputes of this kind, and he is likely to have used many of the ideas and expressions which conventionally belonged to such disputes. The literary form of the *ribh* may well have influenced the composition of the Gospel. But it does not follow from this that the episodes it comprises are altogether unhistorical, either in outline or in detail.

We are led by this route to encounter, once again, what can only be described as a tantalizing ambivalence in the evidence which bears upon the historicity of John's Gospel. In recent years much attention has been paid to the archaeological background of the Gospel. In matters such as place-names, geographical descriptions, religious institutions, and so forth, the author shows a notable degree of precision and accuracy. But what is the implication of this? Either he had access to a tradition of considerable detail and authenticity, and faithfully reproduced it; or he had personal knowledge of these matters, and was therefore able to tell his readers, not how things actually happened, but how they are likely to have happened. That is to say: John's Gospel has been increasingly found to be *plausible*; but evidence of this kind does not help us to decide whether it is *true*.

Precisely the same ambivalence attends the conclusions of our own study. The 'Trial of Jesus', as it stands in the Synoptic Gospels, is an unsatisfactory piece of reporting. Many of the details are implausible, and many important questions remain unanswered. In John's Gospel, the same 'trial' consists of a whole series of encounters between Jesus and the Jewish lawyers, in which the normal procedures for pronouncing the verdict and carrying out the sentence were frustrated again and again by circumstances outside the judges' control. We have seen that, in detail, these encounters correspond very closely with the known conditions of Jewish legal practice, and the tendency of our argument has been to suggest that, of the two accounts (which in any case have important features in common), the Johannine is the more plausible. Yet this in itself does not help us to decide whether the Johannine account is *true*. Indeed, we have suggested that since the author certainly wished to present the case for Jesus in the form of a rehearsal of his 'trial', this must have fundamentally influenced his selection and arrangement of the material about Jesus. The question of how far all this is historical may have been illuminated by our argument: but it will not have been settled.

2. *The milieu of the writer* We have argued that the evangelist was familiar with the conventions and procedures of Jewish litigation; and we have shown grounds for going further than this, and claiming that his mastery of both the detail and the presuppositions of these procedures shows him to have known them, not at second hand, but from the inside. Such an understanding of the application of the Jewish law to the case of one who claimed to be Son of God and Messiah could have been possessed only by a writer steeped in the Jewish culture. To this extent, our argument may be added to the many others which are alleged to show that the author came from, and was steeped in, a distinctly Jewish milieu.

But again, the matter is not so simple.[2] We must not proceed as if only a Jew could be familiar with Jewish law and only a Gentile with Roman or Hellenistic law. We have observed that, though certain features are doubtless peculiar to the Jewish system, there were others which were common to both. Moreover, very few Jews, even in Palestine, would have been familiar only with the Jewish law. The two legal systems existed side by side, and the Gospels themselves provide evidence of Jewish people having recourse to both.

---

[2] Not least because there was not a single or standard Jewish milieu in the last decades of the first century A.D., but rather a considerable variety. The importance of careful study of 'Judaism' at this period is well brought out in C. K. Barrett, *The Gospel of John and Judaism* (1975).

Even the terminology of Gentile courts entered the Jewish vocabulary: we have seen how the idea of the *paraclete*, though strange to the normal practice of the Jewish courts, was adopted into Jewish religious language to describe one of the personages who would appear in the court of heaven. The concept, therefore, of a Jewish milieu, whether in Palestine or in the diaspora, is a somewhat relative one. It may be regarded as likely, as a result of our study, that, to have acquired such an instinctive grasp of Jewish law and Jewish literary forms, the author must have been a Jew, and must have been nurtured in a thoroughly Jewish environment. Yet he is not thereby consigned to a ghetto. On the contrary, his very knowledge of Greek, and of the culture which went with that language, shows him to have belonged to a wider milieu. As was doubtless the case with many other Jewish Christians of his time, his Jewish origin and education by no means circumscribed his interests and his experience, and may even not have been the most distinctive thing about him. It will have enabled him to grasp, as perhaps no Gentile could, the dynamics of the situation created in Jerusalem by the appearance of Jesus. But it will not have prevented him from communicating this understanding in a much more cosmopolitan milieu. One of the most fascinating things about all the Gospels is that they are neither one thing nor the other, neither altogether Jewish nor altogether Gentile, but betwixt and between. And the Fourth is the most betwixt and between of them all.

3. *Destination and purpose of the Gospel* The conclusion to be drawn here is very similar to that of the previous paragraph. Our argument has been that much of the dramatic effect of John's Gospel, and many of its details, depend for their effect upon an understanding of the legal procedures involved. If so, then the Gospel must have been written for people who possessed such an understanding.

But again, our problem is to define who such people may have been. This is a problem which is by no means peculiar to the Fourth Gospel. Consider Paul's letter to the Galatians. The Galatian Christians were under pressure to submit to circumcision. It is certain, therefore, that they were not Jews. Yet much of Paul's argument presupposes a detailed knowledge, not only of the Old Testament, but of technical methods of interpreting the Old Testament. Without such knowledge, its readers or hearers would have been able to make nothing of Paul's reasoning. Who then were these Gentile Christians? We can only suppose that they were people who, through long association with the synagogue, had imbibed enough of Jewish culture and of a basically Jewish outlook for Paul to be able to communicate with them in much the same language and idiom as he used with his fellow-Jews. Once again, we have to imagine a milieu not altogether Jewish nor altogether Gentile, but betwixt and between.

We shall not be far from the truth if we imagine the readers of the Fourth Gospel as belonging to a similarly intermediate culture. Some previous association with the synagogue may be assumed of most of them, whether they were Jews or Gentiles: in the synagogue they will have heard read those passages from Job and the prophets which established the literary convention of great religious issues being argued out as if in a court of law; and through the synagogue they may well have had some opportunity to observe Jewish legal procedures. Thus they will have acquired at least some of the understanding necessary to follow the argument of this Gospel, just as they will have acquired sufficient knowledge of the Old Testament and its interpretation to be able to grasp the sense in which the Scriptures 'witness' to Jesus. There were doubtless both Jews and Gentiles among them: the interest shown in the Greeks who wished to see Jesus (12.21, 23) and in the Jews who had come to believe in Jesus (8.32) suggests that there were both. But again, the Jewishness of this Christian community may well not have been the most significant thing about it. The Gospel which it studied used concepts of far wider provenance than a strictly Jewish culture; and the First Letter of John (which shows no evidence of any first-hand acquaintance with the Old Testament[3]) demonstrates how easily the distinctive Johannine idioms could be used to convey the truths of the Gospel without any borrowing from Jewish sources. Jewishness must have been an important part of its cultural heritage; but it was not the only part.

Were these readers and hearers already Christians? That is to say, was the Gospel intended to be an instrument for spreading the faith, or one for building up the faithful? We have already observed that the author's own statement of his purpose ('that you may believe that Jesus is the Christ, the Son of God'—20.31) fails to answer this question because of an unfortunate uncertainty in the textual tradition: the Greek word meaning 'believe' may be that which means 'come to believe' or that which means 'continue to believe'. But in any case the question deserves to be answered on a wider front; and here at least our argument has a positive contribution to make.

That Jesus is the Christ, the Son of God, is a proposition presented in the Fourth Gospel, not as an established fact, but as an issue on which a judgement is to be passed. The arguments for and against it arise out of the remembered words and deeds of Jesus and may indeed have been developed by Jesus and by his opponents on occasions and along lines similar to those described in the Gospel. But they are also arguments which have still to be weighed by the reader. The verdict reached by Jesus' contemporary judges was not final: the issue is still open, and each reader has to make up his mind.

Was the Gospel therefore a missionary book, addressed to those who had not yet made up their minds about Jesus? But no, even this is too simple. Every Christian records his verdict, not once, but many times. New considerations may cause him to reconsider it, persecution may cause him to retreat from it, new circumstances may invite him to reaffirm it. Again

---

[3] The reference to Cain in 3.12 is to a stock example of villainy, not to any Old Testament passage. cf. A. E. Harvey, *Companion to the NT* (1970), 767.

and again he must review the reasons for which he adheres to it. And in this unending exercise of his own judgement he will find (as Christians and non-Christians alike have found down the centuries) inexhaustible resources in the Gospel according to John.

Index of Passages Cited

BIBLE AND APOCRYPHA

PSEUDEPIGRAPHA, ETC.

RABBINICA

Index of Authors and Subjects